The Sublime and the Beautiful
Irish Art 1700–1830

Edited by William Laffan

THE SUBLIME AND THE BEAUTIFUL
Irish Art 1700 – 1830

Anne Crookshank
The Knight of Glin
Nicola Figgis
Brendan Rooney
Patrick Healy
William Laffan

Edited by William Laffan

Pyms Gallery

FINE ART DEALERS AND VALUERS

9 Mount Street Mayfair London W1K 3NG
Telephone: 020 7629 2020 Facsimile: 020 7629 2060
Email: paintings@pymsgallery.com www.pymsgallery.com

ABBREVIATIONS

The following works have been abbreviated in the footnotes:

Walter Strickland, *A Dictionary of Irish Artists*, 2 Vols, Dublin, 1913, (1969), (Strickland)

Ronald Lightbown (ed.), Anthony Pasquin, [John Williams], *An Authentic History of the Professors of Painting and Architecture who have Practised in Ireland,* London, 1970, (original edition, 1796), (Pasquin)

Anne Crookshank and the Knight of Glin, *The Painters of Ireland, circa 1660 – 1920*, London, 1978, (Crookshank / Glin, 1978)

John Ingamells (ed.), *A Dictionary of British and Irish Travellers in Italy, 1701 – 1800, Compiled from the Brinsley Ford Archive*, New Haven and London, 1997, (Ingamells)

Anne Crookshank, the Knight of Glin, William Laffan, *Masterpieces by Irish Artists, 1660 – 1860*, Pyms Gallery, London, 1999, (Crookshank / Glin / Laffan)

INTRODUCTION AND ACKNOWLEDGMENTS
Alan and Mary Hobart

It is with great pleasure that we present this catalogue and exhibition, our second devoted to Irish art of the eighteenth century. For more than twenty years now Pyms Gallery has pioneered the connoisseurship of Irish painting. When we started handling works by masters such as Orpen, Yeats and Lavery in exhibitions such as *Irish Revival* and *Celtic Splendour* (figures 1 - 2) the mood in London was far from receptive to the promotion of anything Irish and indeed we met with an element of hostility. We like to think that in some small way our efforts over the years have contributed to the esteem in which nineteenth and twentieth-century Irish art is held today. In 1990 we brought our exhibition *A Free Spirit* (figure 3) to the Royal Hibernian Academy in

Figure 1 *Irish Revival,* Pyms Gallery, 1982

Figure 2 *Celtic Splendour,* Pyms Gallery, 1985

6

Dublin, an event which in retrospect can be seen as an important catalyst for the great surge of interest in the subject over the last decade. Our role in stimulating this enthusiasm was acknowledged by an award from the *Irish Post* in 1992 for our contribution to Irish art. As a gallery we have always believed passionately in the primary importance of scholarship in exploring the art of the past. As young dealers we were flattered when the distinguished expert E.H.H. Archibald agreed to write a foreword to our first catalogue devoted to marine painting. Since then we have worked with many leading scholars and published numerous catalogues which have taken their place as invaluable works of reference in their own right. At the end of this catalogue we

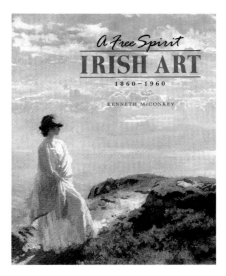

Figure 3 *A Free Spirit,* Pyms Gallery, (in association with the Antique Collectors Club), 1990

include for the first time a full bibliography of our publications and we are gradually putting our more recent catalogues onto our website.

Pyms Gallery is best known for handling works of the nineteenth and twentieth centuries as well as major contemporary artists such as Hector McDonnell. For many years, however, we have also dealt in English and Irish paintings of the eighteenth century including important works by artists such as Reynolds, Gainsborough and Ramsay. The success of our exhibition and catalogue *Irish Masterpieces, 1660 – 1860,* which included works by Roberts, Barret and Fagan demonstrated the renewed interest in Irish painting of this period. At the time we did not think that it would be possible to put together as comprehensive a showing again and indeed the present exhibition is the fruit of two years searching for masterworks of the eighteenth century which as is well known have become increasingly scarce. One of the great advantages of our longevity in business and reputation in the field is that private collectors have the confidence to approach us when they have important paintings to sell.

The next two years will see two important works of scholarship covering the period: Anne Crookshank and the Knight of Glin's *Irish Painting* and the catalogue of the National Gallery of Ireland's eighteenth-century Irish school by Nicola Figgis and Brendan Rooney. We are honoured that all four of these scholars have come together to contribute to this catalogue. Later this year an important exhibition will be held at Kenwood in London charting the collections of the Cobbe Family of Newbridge House while throughout Ireland Georgian houses are being lovingly restored to their original condition and hung with paintings of the period. The new self-confidence in Ireland has allowed a more tolerant view of the material culture of the ascendancy; eighteenth-century Irish Art has found its moment.

In the paintings included in this exhibition we follow the rise of the eighteenth-century school decade by decade: van der Hagen in the 1730s, Collins in the 1740s, Lewis in the 1750s, Forrester and Roberts in the 1760s, Peters in the 1770s and Hamilton and Ashford in the 1780s. We have also included works by James Arthur O'Connor from the early decades of the nineteenth century as we see him as the true heir to artists of the eighteenth-century school such as Roberts - particularly in works such as the *View of Drimnagh Castle* formerly in the collection of Eamonn de Valera. In a pleasing coincidence we show Roberts' greatest work *A Frost Piece* which hung in the same exhibition of the Society of Artists in Ireland in 1769 as Jonathan Fisher's *View of Killarney* which we included in our last catalogue. These two works, though of different landscape genres, sum up the varied strengths of the Irish eighteenth-century school. In the introductory essay Patrick Healy outlines the different approaches to landscape painting open to artists of the period and relates these to the writings of

Edmund Burke from whose famous treatise we have taken this exhibition's title. We are able to illustrate the wealth of Irish landscape paintings with topographical works, capriccios and, in *The Fitzwilliam Forresters*, magnificent essays in the sublime. The exhibition includes a strong group of paintings by Irish artists working in Italy including Fagan, Forrester and Hamilton. Nicola Figgis, the authority on this subject, has kindly written an essay setting these paintings in context. We have included portraits as well as landscapes: Peters' *Portrait of Lady Compton* is, as William Laffan notes in his catalogue entry, perhaps his portrait masterpiece. We are particularly proud to include Turnerelli's marble bust of Henry Grattan one of the greatest Irishmen of the era.

We would like to thank all the contributors to the catalogue. Anne Crookshank and the Knight of Glin, the great pioneers of this subject, have written a very personal essay on their work as well as entries on Roberts and van der Hagen while Brendan Rooney has researched in remarkable detail the history of Irishtown in connection with the painting by James Arthur O'Connor, perhaps one of the most beautiful Dublin views of the age. His entries on the three works by O'Connor present a fresh view of this much-loved artist. We would particularly like to thank Eve McAulay for generously sharing with us her unpublished researches into the Pembroke Estate. The staff of the National Gallery of Ireland, the National Library of Ireland, the National Archives, the Ulster Museum, the National Trust and the Witt Library have been extremely helpful in our repeated requests for information and images. We are also grateful to all the friends and colleagues who have helped in different ways: Professor Kenneth McConkey, Raymond Keaveney, John and Jolanda Cox, Sir Robert and Lady Goff, Fr Anthony Symondson, S.J., Michael Wynne, Hugh Belsey, Christopher Foley, Toby Barnard, Anthony Malcolmson, Evelyne Bell, Anna O'Sullivan and Rachel Withams. Our especial thanks go to William Laffan who has again kindly agreed to edit the catalogue and write the bulk of the entries.

BURKE'S *THE SUBLIME AND THE BEAUTIFUL* AND IRISH LANDSCAPE

Patrick Healy

The tradition of landscape painting in Ireland during the eighteenth century can be divided into three categories; the topographical-antiquarian or loco-descriptive, the picturesque and the romantic sublime. It is in the latter category that the Irish development within the tradition contributes the most original and novel impulse to a wider European scene. The publication of Edmund Burke's *A Philosophical Enquiry into the Origins of our Ideas of the Sublime and the Beautiful*, gave the age a comprehensive theoretical text that not only charts an important shift in *mentalité*, but also creates a bulwark for the new emotional and expressive concerns of Irish landscape art. Such is the achievement of artists directly inspired by Burke, or immediately patronised by him, such as Barrett, Barry, Forrester, that Ireland has become synonymous with the concept of landscape, nature, scenery, and much of the lexis of the sublime is transferred in literary epithets to the country, haunting, wild, rugged, majestic, mysterious, such that, as late as 1835, John O'Donovan conducting research for the Ordnance Survey, hiding behind a rock and listening to the swell of the Tory Sound declared that this was the 'sublime' of Edmund Burke. To this day Sean Fingelton of Donegal and the Tory Island school, inspired by Derek Hill, maintain compelling variations on this tradition. Paradoxically the pictures which made this seeing of Ireland possible, become less and less visible because of the success of their artistic aims.

In the *Enquiry* Burke makes a telling criticism, of the limitations of topographical imitation;

> If I make a drawing of a palace, or a temple, or a landscape, I present a very clear idea of those objects, but then (allowing for the effect of imitation which is something) my picture can at most affect only as the palace, temple, or landscape would have affected it in the reality. (pp. 101 – 2)

Burke sees topographical imitation as inhibiting the imagination. Burke has in mind the loco-descriptive approach which Anne Crookshank and the Knight of Glin have identified in works of Dirk Maas, Willem van der Hagen and specifically Francis Place, a friend of Hollar, whose pen and ink drawings, often made on the spot, bring the northern European tradition of 'landscape of fact' to Ireland. It might, however, be observed that the use of such detailed topography when allied with antiquarian interests are often much less realistic than they seem. The specific Dutch seventeenth-entury practices which were imported to Ireland in the wake of the campaigns of William III, attempting plausible re-creations of scenes, depend on strong artistic conventions and supply very specific needs. It is the artistic conventions that have become naturalised, and the artlessness and informal quality of representation often overcomes any verisimilitude. Place's view of Kilkenny Castle is a good example, and his bird's eye views of Waterford and Drogheda exemplify the need for a sense of stability in the new settler world.

Nevertheless the limitations of such showing was felt and a more sophisticated viewing public required a different response to the 'soft primitivism' of much of the literary depiction of Ireland in the works of writers such as Boate, Stanihurst and Molyneux. Molyneux who had been fascinated to look at painted miniature portraits through a microscope, had noted that there was a pleasing prospect of Kilkenny Castle from a bridge on the River Nore. A good prospect and a single viewpoint had even at this date a therapeutic value, as advertised in Burton's anatomy of melancholy. The acculturation of nature required a sense of the typical place. In van der Hagen's Carrickfergus scene, the painting functions also as a commemorative site, it was the landing place of William of Orange.

In van der Hagen's work there are multiple stylistic responses to landscape, it is also possible that his activity as a scene painter for the theatre freed his imagination to create capriccios, which are so important to the Venetian tradition for the production of views. The specific impulse for scenography had been discussed by Serlio as allowing for a free movement of *fantasia* especially with regard to ruins. Thus even in the whiggish neo-Burlington Palladianism, developed in Ireland, departure from rules and the ordering of the arts was permissible. The function of landscape as defined by Blount in the mid-seventeenth century, a kind of by-way in a picture, something incidental, a parergon, comes to be a complete subject in theatre scenography in the eighteenth century. The full absorption of the idiom of the Dutch-Italianate capriccio can be seen in the work of Robert Carver, where also the direct lesson of Claude has been learnt.

In the second category of landscape - the picturesque, one detects a new sophisticating of visual experience and consumption of pictorial images. Literally there was the creation of an artifice where one lived 'as in a picture'. Indeed Burke thinks that the notion of proportion of beauty in architecture is a form of pathic, platonised projection onto nature, but notes "nature has at last escaped from their discipline and their fetters, and our gardens, if nothing else, declare, we begin to feel, that mathematical ideas are not the true measure of beauty". Burke is objecting to the domesticising and controlling of nature. "Therefore having observed, that their dwellings were most commodious and firm when they were thrown into regular figures, with parts answerable to each other; they transferred these ideas to their gardens; they turned their trees into pillars, pyramids, and obelisks; they formed their hedges into so many green walls, and fashioned the walks into squares, triangles and other mathematical figures, with exactness and symmetry" (p. 183 - 84). Burke is providing a sharp critique of the regnant idea that the beauty of proportion in architecture is based on the human body and secondly signalling his awareness that the development in garden art has loosened up the relation to the natural world. It points to the development of the picturesque and furnishes a subtending criticism, that just as the topographical is not realistic the picturesque is not natural.

The picturesque emerged from the wish to confirm the edifying nature of travel, involving a refined control of the emotions, where characteristic moments are selected and the choice of viewpoint is one which favours the framing of the natural spectacle in a picture. One can say that the picturesque coincides with the development of a society of display. This is apparent in Ireland in the proliferation of new subjects from the late 1730s of a society at play, consuming pleasure, pictures of balls, parties, creations of a beau walk, the development within portraiture of the self consciousness of commemorative likeness and showing of social luxury. In Burke's sense these are the passions of society which he sets against nature, very much as he contrasts the beautiful with the sublime. The increased need for controllable pictures and the self-conscious construction of life lived in a pictorial, scenographic way is beautifully parodied in Swift's *Polite Conversation*. It is in the work of Mrs Delany and the activities of Lord Kenmare that one can fully explore the picturesque in Ireland, the beginning also of the history of 'tourism'. But it is the Grand Tour that contributes to the end of this very preference. Where internal travel in Ireland had led to the cultivation of the picturesque, travel in the form of the Grand Tour, undertaken by Berkeley, Milltown and Charlemont led to the discovery of *grandeur,* which for Burke is always directly related to the poetry of Milton, a fascination that is ruggedly pursued by James Barry throughout his artistic life.

The shift in *mentalité* is fully gathered in the text of Burke, and gives insight into the pictures that are described as romantic, gothic and sublime or Kenneth Clark's 'graveyard school'. Burke's direct influence on Barry and Barrett is well recorded, both painting as it were pendants to his text. It became prescriptive. Bishop Berkeley had been one of the first to speak of the pleasing horror at the idea of the depths of the ocean or the experience of an overwhelming mountain or a dark primeval forest. Burke's *Enquiry* is an attempt to give an empirical psychological account of astonishment. The enigma of the dread and unknowability of God. The principle of the sublime is 'terror'. By the investigation of a speculative psychology which reaffirms the pathos of mystery, Burke advances another relationship to nature, and to human nature. Darkness and mystery are necessary, they evoke the uncanny, the dark and the obscure. Man is the middle term between nature and God, and *pace* Milton 'the mind is its own place'. For Burke a clear idea is a little idea. It is a terrible uncertainty which is germane to the sublime, the grand cause of terror he argues is 'wrapped up in the shades of its own incomprehensible darkness' (p. 109). Burke wants to distinguish between society and nature. Nature is overpowering and overwhelming. The overpowering and the overwhelming in nature provoke the fear and dread in which because of the power of pain, the work of art is a form of self-preservation, a dealing with the fear provoked.

Burke moves away from the complacency of the loco-descriptive tradition in some ways the staid rational geometry of the Georgian world-view. His is a radiant notion of sublimity. Darkness visible, the storms at sea, the terror, pain, angst, dread, - a whole new lexis, that moves away from rational control of nature, from the idea of the external spectacle of nature as being picturesque, or indeed as being able to maintain the concept of the analogy of the rightness of creation. For Burke whatever excites the ideas of pain and danger, or is analogous to terror, is a source of the sublime, productive of the strongest emotions of which the mind is capable (p. 59). He challenges the artist to understand the power of nature, and the psychological issue of how there is a delight in contemplating danger. The pursuit of feeling, and emotion become paramount on the side of the subject.

But Burke has also prescriptive advice; danger and the sublime are maintained by obscurity. Pictures need to learn from words where rhetorical effect and the ability to convey the affections of the mind from one to another is achieved in the shades of 'its own incomprehensible darkness' (p. 109). However Burke wants the artist to avoid 'odd wild grotesques' and comments that 'all the designs I have chanced to meet of the temptation of St Anthony, were rather a sort of wild grotesque, than anything capable of producing a serious passion' (p. 109). The serious passion Burke requires is to be like the sacred and reverential awe with regard to divinity, the notion of a thesphanic power is for him 'a capital source of the sublime'. In unfinished sketches of drawings 'I have often seen something which pleased me beyond the best finishing', and comments on Stonehenge that it may not have anything admirable in disposition or ornament, but that the very rudeness of the work increases the cause of grandeur (p. 139). Darkness is more productive of sublime ideas than light (p. 145) and the sublime abhors mediocrity (p. 147). Burke wants painters to imagine scenes which as Walpole once remarked of Piranesi 'would startle geometry'. Grand images he contends cannot be produced by soft and cheerful colours. "An immense mountain covered with a shining green turf is nothing in this respect to one dark and gloomy; the cloudy sky is more grand than the blue; and night more sublime and solemn than day" (p. 149).

No one responded more directly to these passages of Burke than his fellow Dubliner

James Forrester, who would make a speciality of night scenes, in which a reverential awe is the dominating mood (see catalogue 5 - 6). The interest in sepulchral monuments had first brought Piranesi to Charlemont's attention in Rome. Clearly painting darkness responds to one of the deepest interests in Burke's *Enquiry*, and in the second edition he added considerable material on darkness and the sublime, taking issue with Locke, (p. 272 - 286) coupled with his more specific observation.

> And I think there are reasons in nature why this obscure idea, when properly conveyed, should be more affecting than the clear...The ideas of eternity and infinity, are among the most affecting we have, and yet perhaps there is nothing which we really understand so little.

Burke quotes Milton's portrait of Satan, "we do not anywhere meet a more sublime description 'He above the rest in shape and gesture proudly eminent...'" which succeeds because of what Burke calls obscureness. A quality even more important in painting: "but painting, when we have allowed for the "leisure of imitation, can only affect simply by the images it presents, and even in painting a judicious obscurity in some things contributes to the effect of the picture, because the images have a greater power on the fancy to form the grander passions than those have which are more clear and determinate" (p. 107).

For Burke 'a clear idea is a little idea'. It is a terrible uncertainty which is germane to the sublime. Burke quotes the 'amazingly sublime' passage in the Book of Job, "In thoughts from the visions of the night, when deep sleep falleth upon men, fear came upon me and trembling, which made all my bones to shake...an image was before mine eyes; there was silence; and I heard a voice - shall mortal man be more just than God". Astonishment is the effect of the sublime in the highest degree; the inferior effects are admiration, reverence and respect (p. 96). Fear being an apprehension of pain or death resembles actual pain. The scale of the size of the provoking object is not in question. Obscurity adds to this effect. The druids performed their ceremonies in "the bosom of the darkest woods, and in the shade of the eldest most spreading oaks" (p. 100). Burke quotes Milton's description of death:

> The other shape
> If shape it might be called that shape had none
> Distinguishable, in member, joint or limb.

Perhaps this is the terror and enigma which lies at the heart of Burke's sublime, the riddle and the secret which is set against the shape that had none, and whose lack of distinction makes fearful and astonishes.[1]

---

1   I have used the second edition of *A Philosophical Enquiry*, (1759), which includes extensive revisions of the first edition of 1757. For these revisions see H.A. Wichelns "Burke's Essay on the Sublime and its Reviewers" in *Journal of English and Germanic Philology*, Vol. 21, pp 645 - 61. For the concept of *mentalité* see Michele Vovelle, *Ideologies and Mentalities*, translated by E.O'Flaherty, London, 1990. For the concept of the loco-descriptive see John Barrell, *The Idea of Landscape and the Sense of Place*, 1730 – 1840, Cambridge, 1977. Molyneux's comments are cited by Ehrenpreis in the first volume of his trilogy on Swift. For the specific Dutch antecedents of Irish topographical landscape see *Beelden van een Strijd* an exhibition at the Het Prinsenhof, Delft, March – June 1998. For the influence of Burke on British artists among whom Cozens, Patch and Turner together with the influence of Poussin, Rosa, Dughet etc see Luke Herrmann, *British Landscape Painting of the 18th Century*, London, 1973 where the importance of Vernet and his Irish wife is discussed. For the Graveyard School see Kenneth Clark, *The Gothic Revival*, London, 1962. James Stevens Curl in his *Art and Architecture of Freemasonry*, London, 1991, discusses thinking about death, cenotaphs and cemeteries.

IRISH ARTISTS IN ROME IN THE EIGHTEENTH CENTURY

Nicola Figgis

In the eighteenth century the magnetism of Italy was strong for artists from Ireland. This was in part due to the enthusiasm of writers of guide books like Joseph Addison (1672 - 1719), who described Italy as the 'great school of music and painting' and as possessing 'the noblest productions of statuary and architecture, both ancient and modern'.[2] Such an enticement would have appealed to pupils of the Dublin Society Schools, who were introduced to classical art by drawing casts of antique statues and by copying engravings after the classical landscapes of Claude Lorrain and Gaspard Dughet.

Those heading for Italy set off on what was sometimes an arduous journey. Matthew William Peters (see catalogue 9) wrote of the length of time it took to sail in a small ship from Dublin to Italy:

> I am but a week in Rome though I left Dublin last August, having been two months at sea between that place and Cadiz, beating about in the midst of the equinoctial storms on board a little one-masted Dutch dogger.[3]

In September 1766 James Barry (1741 - 1806), a devotee of Edmund Burke's aesthetic theories, enjoyed the sublime experience of travelling overland via the Alps, describing 'the most awful and horridly grand, romantic, and picturesque scenes'.[4] In November 1739, Horace Walpole (1717 - 97) had been the first traveller to appreciate the picturesque quality of the Alps. Pulling up the blinds of his carriage he exclaimed

---

2   Joseph Addison, *Remarks on Several Parts of Italy*, London, 1705, p. 1
3   W.T. Whitley, *Artists and their Friends in England*, London, 1928, Vol. I, p. 305
4   James Barry, *The Works of James Barry*, (E. Fryer ed.), London, 1809, Vol. I, pp. 58 - 59. For further discussion of this subject see the essay by Patrick Healy above.

'wolves howling, torrents, precipices, Salvator Rosa'.[5] Generally travellers found this passage terrifying, preferring to keep the blinds firmly down on their carriages until forced to look when they disembarked at Mont Cenis and were carried up the steeper slopes in a type of sedan chair. Probably shivering with cold and fright, they must have consoled themselves with the promise of the warmth and tranquillity of the Roman Campagna.

Having completed the journey to Rome, they entered from the north side of the city by the Via Flaminia into the Piazza del Popolo. British and Irish travellers tended to stay in the area around the Piazza di Spagna. In the eighteenth century the Piazza became known as the *Ghetto degli Inglesi* and the *Caffé degli Inglesi* was the central meeting place. Grand Tourists stayed in the immediate vicinity of the Piazza, which was more expensive. Artists and dealers like Robert Fagan (see catalogue 12) who had the means, lived near to the Piazza di Spagna on the Via del Babuino in the Palazzo Piombino. In 1783 Hugh Douglas Hamilton (see catalogue 8) stayed off the Piazza di Spagna in the Casa Mignanelli.

Generally artists tended to take less expensive lodgings in houses on the Pincian Hill, in the area immediately south of the Trinità dei Monti, which from 1726 was linked to the Piazza di Spagna by the Spanish Steps or *Scalinata*. From this aspect there were delightful views overlooking Rome. The Palazzo Zuccari, situated on the Via Gregoriana (today the Hertziana Library) was traditionally a home for artists and the Irish landscape painters, Solomon Delane (circa 1727 - 1812) and Edmund Garvey (*fl.* 1764 - 1813) stayed there while in Rome. To the rear, the Palazzo Zuccari faces on to the Strada Felice (today the Via Sistina), where Hugh Douglas Hamilton lived in 1784; from 1786 to 1792 he stayed nearby in a street leading uphill off the Strada Felice, at the Casa Guarnieri.

---

5   H. Walpole, *The Yale Edition of Horace Walpole's Correspondence*, W.S. Lewis (ed.), New Haven, 1948, Vol. XIII, p. 181

In the eighteenth century visiting artists were intent on improving their knowledge of antiquity, in order to raise the status of their work. Rome provided incomparable opportunities for the study of antique statues, principally those belonging to the Vatican at the Palazzo dei Conservatori on the Capitoline Hill and at the Belvedere Courtyard. In 1733 Clement XII acquired a collection of antiquities donated by Cardinal Alessandro Albani (1692 - 1779). This formed the basis of a new museum on the Capitol, which opened in 1734. In Bramante's Belvedere Courtyard, some of the most important antique statues were placed, such as the *Laocoön* and the *Apollo Belvedere*. Up until 1770 viewing of the statues in the Belvedere Courtyard was restricted to larger pieces but in that year other works in the collection as well as newly acquired sculptures became accessible to the public. Clement XIV (1769 - 1774) opened a museum of antique sculpture at the Vatican which was extended under his successor Pius VI (1774 - 1799) and became known as the Museo Pio-Clementino.

Early in the eighteenth century during the papacy of Clement XI (1700 - 21), foreign students were encouraged to enter competitions at the Academia di S. Luca, Rome's most prestigious academy of art. The Irish artist Henry Trench (circa 1685 - 1726) was awarded several prizes by the Academy, firstly in 1705 for red chalk drawings of statues of *Bacchus, Apollo* and *Cleopatra*, then in the private collection of the Giustiniani family. Other award winning drawings by him included *The Slaying of Tarpeia* (1706) and *Furius Camillus and the Teacher* (1711).[6]

Attached to the Capitoline Museum, a school of life drawing, known as the Accademia del Nudo, was founded by Benedict XIV in 1754. Classes were free of charge and were given by members of the Accademia di S. Luca, like Giovanni Panini (1691 - 1765), Anton Raphael Mengs (1728 - 79), Pompeo Batoni (1708 - 87), Anton von Maron (1733 - 1808) and Vicenzo Pacetti (1746 - 1820). Between 1755 and 1769 eighty-nine foreigners were registered as attending,[7] including the Irish artists Jacob Ennis (1728 -

---

6   Nicola Figgis, 'Henry Trench (circa 1685 - 1726): Painter and Illustrator', in *Irish Arts Review Yearbook,* 1994, pp. 217 - 22

7   M.F. MacDonald, 'British Artists at the Academia del Nudo in Rome', in *Academies of Art,* Leiden, 1989, pp. 77 - 94

70), who was awarded a prize there in 1755, Robert Crone (circa 1718 - 79) and Matthew William Peters. On 6 May 1762, Peters wrote

> At the Pope's Academy, where I attend, the human figure is every day in the week, (holidays excepted), free for any person to draw after without any expense - in the summer at half an hour after five in the morning and in winter after nightfall - two hours each time; near which are many large galleries erected for pictures and statues, where people may at any time study, but it has this disadvantage, that the pictures are not allowed to be taken down nor scaffolds to be made. The light, however, is very good and as well contrived as possible for the benefit of study.[8]

Red chalk life studies were executed by James Barry and James Forrester while in Rome. They must have attended life classes either at the Academia del Nudo or the French Academy in the Villa Mancini on the Corso, founded by Louis XIV in 1666. The French Academy provided facilities for artists of all nationalities to take life classes and to study its notable collection of casts after the antique. These casts took on greater significance when originals began to leave collections in Rome; from as early as 1738 statues from the Farnese collection, inherited by Charles III, left for Naples and much of the Medici collection was moved to Florence from the early 1770s.

Among the many Irish artists who benefited from their studies of antique statuary, were Hugh Douglas Hamilton and Robert Fagan. Hamilton is known for his oval portraits in pastel of such sitters as James Colyear Dawkins (catalogue 8), as well as for larger pastels of sitters seen full length against Roman ruins (figure 4). In the case of a second portrait of Dawkins, he is shown beside a Roman sarcophagus seemingly at the Villa Albani (figure 30). Hamilton also produced a subject painting in oils in Rome, entitled *Diana and Endymion* (1783; private collection). The two figures were borrowed from a Hellenistic relief of Endymion as well as a section of the *Gerontia Sarcophagus* on

---

8   Whitley, *op. cit.*, Vol. I, p. 306

Figure 4 Hugh Douglas Hamilton, *Portrait of Jonas Langford Brooke*, private collection

Figure 5 Robert Fagan, *A Portrait of Sir Andrew Corbet Corbet and his wife Hester with a view of the Temple of Minerva Medica*, private collection

display at the Capitoline Museum.[9] On return to Dublin, the idea for his painting *Cupid and Psyche* (1792 - 3, National Gallery of Ireland) was influenced by the antique sculptures of the same pair both at the Capitoline and in the Tribuna of the Uffizi, as well as by the neo-classical sculptor, Antonio Canova (1757 - 1822). Hamilton's admiration of Canova's *modello* of his own *Cupid and Psyche* is celebrated in his pastel portrait of the sculptor in his studio with the Irish artist, Henry Tresham (circa 1788 - 89; Victoria and Albert Museum, London) (figure 29).

As well as painting the elegant portraits of visiting grand-tourists for which he is best known such as figure 5, between 1792 and 1795, Robert Fagan painted seventeen grisaille panels after antique sculpture, which were acquired by Thomas Noel Hill, 2nd Baron Berwick (1770 - 1832) for Attingham Park, Shropshire. Some of these were based on sculptures at the Capitoline Museum, others from the Villa Albani, Rome, the Bourbon collection in Naples and the Uffizi, which he may have copied at the French Academy (see figure 44). Fagan was also an archaeologist. His enthusiasm for sculpture reveals itself in his oil paintings, like the *Self-portrait* (Hunt Museum, Limerick), where his second wife is presented in grey tones, inviting the viewer to make comparisons with sculptures like the *Campo Iemini Venus*, which he himself had excavated.[10]

Sketching or copying paintings by Italian masters, from the High Renaissance onwards, was a useful exercise for artists. Studying the frescoes of Michelangelo and Raphael at the Vatican was of primary importance and encouraged by Sir Joshua Reynolds in his *Discourses*. In September 1768, James Barry wrote that he had made two copies after Raphael at the Villa Farnesina and that he had started copying Titian's *Three Graces* and *The Adoration of the* Shepherds at the Villa Borghese, in order to try and learn something of the Venetian artist's use of colour.[11] Matthew William Peters wrote 'I shall

9 Fintan Cullen, 'Hugh Douglas Hamilton in Rome', in *Apollo*, Vol. 115, 1982, p. 89

10 Ilaria Bignamini, 'The "Campo Iemini Venus" Rediscovered', *Burlington Magazine*, Vol. 136, August 1994, p. 552. See Nicola Figgis and Brendan Rooney, 'Robert Fagan', *Paintings of the Irish School*, National Gallery of Ireland, Vol. I, forthcoming (October 2001)

11 James Barry, *op. cit.*, Vol. I, p. 119

look after the Old Masters for those things that require most study.'[12] In Florence he produced a copy of Titian's *Venus d'Urbino* at the Uffizi.[13] According to Manners, Peters was later referred to as the 'English Titian' because of his series of portraits of reclining ladies, inspired by this painting.[14] Some of these paintings were mildly erotic, such as *Sylvia, a Courtesan* (National Gallery of Ireland), unlike his very refined portrait of Lady Elizabeth Compton (catalogue 9) in full elegant dress.

Copies of much admired works were often acquired by visiting collectors, attested to by the many paintings after works such as Guido Reni's *Aurora* (Palazzo Rospigliosi, Rome), Raphael's *Madonna della Sedia* (Pitti Palace, Florence) as well as Titian's *Venus d'Urbino* already mentioned. The Bishop of Derry had two copies of Raphael's *School of Athens* in his collection for galleries in two of his houses. Correggio's *Madonna of St. Jerome* proved one of Parma's major attractions and Peters' copy may now be seen in the Parish Church of Saffron Walden, Essex. In Perugia Peters copied the *Madonna della Scudella* by Federico Barocci (circa 1535 - 1612) as commissioned by the 1st Baron Clive (1725 - 74).

The influence of contemporary foreign painters in Rome was also significant. The French landscape painter, Claude-Joseph Vernet (1714 - 89), first came to Rome in 1734 and remained there for sixteen years, living in an apartment with a studio at the Palazzo Zuccari. Vernet, inspired by the landscapes of Claude Lorrain, is best known for his marine paintings, showing different times of the day, such as the series ordered by Robert Wood for Joseph Leeson in 1749 (Beit collection).[15] Following Vernet's example, James Forrester also painted views shown at various times of day as well as during the night; in 1771 he painted two scenes of *Moonlight* and *Morning* for his patron, Henry Belling, 8th Baron Arundell of Wardour (1740 - 1808), which were much admired. On completion of these works, he was commissioned by Arundell to paint

12 Whitley, *op. cit.*, Vol. I, p. 306
13 Lady Victoria Manners, *Matthew William Peters, R.A., His Life and Work*, London, 1913, p. 3
14 *Ibid.*, p. 6
15 See Sergio Benedetti, *The Milltowns: a Family Reunion*, National Gallery of Ireland, Dublin, 1997, pp. 88 - 91

two further scenes, showing a sunrise and a sunset.[16]

The Welsh landscape painter, Richard Wilson (1713 - 82), who also emulated the style of Claude, was himself a source of inspiration. Wilson stayed in Rome from 1751 to 1757 and during that time taught a former pupil of the Dublin Society Schools, Robert Crone.[17] Two landscapes by Crone after Wilson were sold in the auction rooms of James Vallence, 6 Eustace Street in 1803, formerly the property of 'the late Alexander Mangin and William Ashford, Esq. a privy councellor'.[18]

It was too hot to be in Rome during the summer months and artists like Wilson moved to cooler neighbourhoods like Tivoli and the Alban Hills, dotted with Roman ruins and redolent of the poetry of Virgil. Wilson's scenes were often melancholic, reflecting on the passed Golden Age of Rome. Forrester's views which include Roman remains are similar in tone and reflect on the passage of time from antiquity. Virgilian associations with these sites inspired paintings with underlying mythological themes, such as Forrester's paintings of Lake Nemi, Virgil's *Speculum Dianae* (catalogue 6).

Wilson's more romantic style of painting, exemplified by *The Destruction of the Children of Niobe*, (figure 22) can be seen in Forrester's painting of a stormy scene (catalogue 5). During a trip from Rome in 1769, which lasted eighteen days, during which they sometimes travelled by moonlight in order to avoid the heat of the day, Forrester often focused on the more romantic elements of the journey. At Terni he described a waterfall, which may have been the subject of one of his drawings acquired that year by John Dawson, 1st Earl of Portarlington (Victoria and Albert Museum, London) (figure 6).

We had a ride, romantic beyond imagination, to the top of the cascade,

---

16 Paul Mellon Centre for Studies in British Art, the Brinsley Ford Archive, London. See calendar of letters from Father John Thorpe in Rome to the 8th Baron Arundell.

17 N. Figgis, 'Irish Landscapists in Rome 1750 - 1780', in *Irish Arts Review*, Vol. 4, No. 4, Winter 1987, pp. 60 - 62

18 Burton Fredericksen, *Index of Paintings Sold in the British Isles During the Nineteenth Century*, Vol. I, p. 218; May 1803 (lots 89 and 90)

which is dreadful to behold: below us appeared a most brilliant rainbow, to which the dark, moist and mossy rocks were an excellent foil. This wonderful water-fall attracted our attention for nearly two hours, until the heat rendered our long stay intolerable.[19]

This drawing makes an interesting comparison with Forrester's early drawing of the waterfall at Powerscourt (Ulster Museum) (figure 7) neatly linking the quest for the sublime in Italy and Ireland.

Forrester's excursion continued to Spoleto and Foligno and he describes the dangers of travel in a storm which they encountered, which seems to have been an even more sublime experience than that shown in his painting of 1766 (catalogue 5).

> There arose one of the most dreadful storms of thunder, hail, wind and rain, that I was ever witness of, and which continued without intermission for a full hour. The imminent danger of our situation increased the horror of the dreadful sight; the road narrow, being open on the left-hand to a tremendous precipice, deeper than the height of the cupola of St Peter's, without the least fence. From this danger we escaped under the providence of God by the unconcernedness of the mules, which withstood all the terrors of the storm.

The educational value of a trip to Italy cannot be over-estimated, in spite of the fact that Edmund Burke insisted to George Barret that he would learn more from the landscapes of County Wicklow, a point perhaps exemplified by Forrester's drawings of the waterfalls of Terni and Powerscourt. Artists like Jacob Ennis and Barry returned home equipped with their own casts of antique statues and others like Hamilton brought back sketches and prints that they had collected in Italy. A visit of at least a year was recommended for a Grand Tour but artists tended to stay for longer periods. Some like Peters returned to Italy for a second visit; others like Forrester and Fagan could not bear to tear themselves away and remained in Italy permanently.

---

19 James Forrester, *Tour of Italy in the Year 1769*, London, 1787, p. 10

Figure 7 James Forrester, *Powerscourt Waterfall*,
Photograph reproduced with the kind
permission of the Trustees of the Museums
& Galleries of Northern Ireland

Figure 6 James Forrester, *Waterfall at Terni*,
Victoria and Albert Museum,
V&A Picture Library

REFLECTIONS ON AND MEMORIES OF IRISH PAINTING

Anne Crookshank and Desmond FitzGerald, Knight of Glin

Anne Crookshank's return to Ireland from her career in the Tate and the Witt Library of the Courtauld Institute occurred in 1957 when she took up the position of Keeper of Art in the Belfast Museum and Art Gallery, which became the Ulster Museum and has recently become known as the Museums and Galleries of Northern Ireland (MAGNI). She found that the largest sum of money ever spent on a picture was 250 pounds on a Peter de Wint watercolour: that there was no regular budget for purchasing or for exhibitions. She went through the pictures finding a fine small collection of English works of the 20s and 30s, artists such as Augustus John, and Stanley Spencer, and a few contemporary Irish works such as, O'Rorke Dickey, Paul Henry, Humbert Craig and Louis Le Brocquy.

There were too an extraordinarily varied group of old masters, a Turner, eight very fine Fuseli drawings, and one or two Italian and Dutch paintings, mostly unattributed, some later to be attributed by her such as the two of seated boys, one holding vegetables and the other a dog, by the Bergamesque painter Giacamo Ceruti. There was a James Arthur O'Connor and a Panini to give some idea of the *mixsom gatherum*. She then sent a report to the committee containing the facts and pointing out that without regular money and an acquisition policy the museum would never flourish and that good paintings, even then, usually cost more that 250 pounds. Luckily at that moment a full length Lawrence, not one of his best, but of the Countess of Belfast, came on the market for 1,000 pounds and they agreed to buy it and to try and get a regular income. This rose steadily over the 7 years she was there to 14,000 pounds but of course it had to deal with all the departments of art, i.e. silver, ceramics, costume and a small sum for old masters in an effort to make the few available more cohesive.

Michael Levey of the National Gallery, London was most helpful in finding works within our means.

This was a great start and she found the then Duke of Abercorn who became Chairman when the Museum was taken over some years later by the State and called the Ulster Museum, was sympathetic, interested and willing to accept that with few resources buying modern art was a good financial expedient. As a result with the help of Ronald Alley of the Tate, she was able to draw up a good varied list of artists which would show the different shades of modern art and he remained an immensely helpful supporter who found works for us in London. The City Council recoiled with horror at what she was buying and at one of their meetings referred to her as the Whore of Babylon. From her point of view the new arrangements when they came were a great improvement. A group of the committee used to come to London on buying sprees. She always found that they liked to choose from two or three works and by the end of the day they were so exhausted that the Duke, when safely in his taxi, would lean out of the window saying "I don't mind what you buy now so long as none of us have to see any of them". We bought very little Irish because we were unfamiliar with the artists, we got a few English but mostly Continental or even American, Peter Lanyon, Dubuffet, Appel, Kenneth Noland, Tapies, Uecker, Sam Francis, Helen Frankenthaler, William Scott and Jack Yeats, (rare Irish purchases) and a number of others.

Anne was always aware of her sad lack of knowledge of Irish painters of all periods and she found to her misfortune that she never knew the names of any of the artists whose pictures hung on the walls of the houses she visited. Probably in 1957 or 1958 when spending a weekend in Donegal she met and made friends with Desmond and Mariga Guinness who had just founded the Irish Georgian Society. Through them she met Desmond FitzGerald who was a post-graduate student in the Fine Arts Department at Harvard and spent his summer vacations in Ireland. As a group in 1963 they formed the idea, with the help of James White who later became first the Curator of the Municipal Gallery and finally Director of the National Gallery of Ireland, of arranging an exhibition *Irish Houses and Landscapes*. This aimed at showing landscapes which included houses, a subject in which the two Desmonds were particularly interested. It also connected with the research that Desmond FitzGerald was engaged in, writing his thesis on Irish Palladianism.

The extent of our ignorance was such that a panoramic view of Glin, which we brightly described as J.H. Brocas, was discovered, after cleaning for the exhibition by Alexander Dunluce, to be signed and dated J.H. Mulcahy, 1839 - a Limerick painter of whom we had never heard. It was too late to reposition it in the catalogue under M, where it should have been. We were also very uncertain about two brothers called Thomas Roberts, we could not believe that two brothers would have the same name, but we went along with Strickland,[20] the bible of Irish art history, and five years later, or even more, Edward McParland, the great Irish architectural historian found the letter from Roberts' great niece which told the story that Sautell Roberts took his brother's Christian name after his tragic early death.

Anne moved to Dublin at the very end of 1965 having got the post in Trinity College, to set up a History of Art Department. She had decided that despite endless exhibitions, lecture series and every sort of enticement there were very few more people coming to the museum than before. She felt that education was absolutely essential. Desmond had become an Assistant Keeper in the arcanely termed Department of Furniture and Woodwork in the Victoria and Albert Museum. *Irish Portraits 1660 - 1860* (figure 8) was the next venture of Desmond (with the forbearance of his Keeper, Peter Thornton) and Anne with James White and Michael Wynne, his assistant in the National Gallery, and under the enthusiastic chairmanship

20 Walter Strickland, *Dictionary of Irish Artists*, 2 Vols, Dublin, 1913

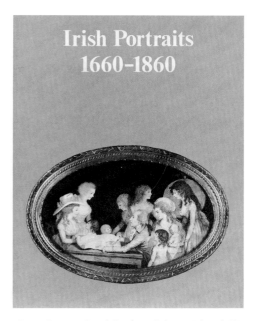

Figure 8 Anne Crookshank and the Knight of Glin, *Irish Portraits 1660 – 1860*, London, 1969

of Roy Strong of the National Portrait Gallery in London. This exhibition was ready by 1969 for showing in London and in 1970 in Dublin and later in Belfast. It was a far more serious and professional effort in comparison with the somewhat amateurish *Irish Houses and Landscapes*. However, these two catalogues were the foundation for our later researches.

After *Portraits* Anne was asked to write a book on Irish art but she felt that, given the amount of work it would take, Desmond would have to be involved. He found another publisher, Barrie and Jenkins, who were in less of a hurry and were prepared to wait a few years and he also found a patron, Timothy Gwyn-Jones who nobly subsidised the illustrations. This eventually evolved into the first general book on Irish painting from the seventeenth to the early twentieth century and was entitled *The Painters of Ireland* published in 1978. The production of this book was not without incident. A major bout of depression followed by manic energy by Desmond not to mention an acute attack of gout while we were proof-reading, leaving Anne in the car park reading and Desmond in the Adelaide Hospital out-patients also reading, and at the last minute Anne went down with cancer. Of course she recovered just in time for the launch in the National Gallery, when an over excited Desmond verbally attacked Forbes Singer, who owned Barrie and Jenkins at the time, for stopping the drinks at 8 o'clock! In those early days Anne and Desmond used to fight ferociously about attributions. Desmond would rush out of the room, slam the door and pace round New Square in Trinity until he had cooled down to find a sullen Anne working away. Good humour returned remarkably quickly and there was no sulking! The attributions were finally resolved and age has softened our temperaments.

But to return to the work. Lisa van Gruisen helped us with our photographic forays round many a country house collection in Ireland and these photographs became the basis of our archive which has been the essential tool behind our research. We also pounded round the Lowlands of Scotland and all over England chasing up the descendants of Lords Lieutenants and of the aristocracy and gentry, many of whom had left Ireland in the last 100 years. The piecing together of Ireland's artists took quite a lot of luck and imagination. For instance a beautiful portrait of Bishop Berkeley in Trinity College, which was known to be by James Latham through a mezzotint, reminded Desmond of a double portrait of two ladies of the Leslie family by a harpsichord playing Handel, which he had known very well as a child as the Leslies were his next door neighbours at Glin. From this beginning over a hundred portraits have been found and Latham established as the finest portrait painter of the first half of the eighteenth century. The finest landscape painter, Thomas Roberts, who we have already mentioned, was almost as elusive as Latham. We worked, however, in parallel with Michael Wynne who did a small exhibition of his work in the gallery, and who with Cynthia O'Connor was the only other serious toiler in this eighteenth-century Irish field. It is pleasant to record that the *festschrift* dedication to Michael on Lord Charlemont has just been published with a memoir of Cynthia O'Connor.[21]

Ellis K. Waterhouse in his *Dictionary of British 18th Century Painters* (1981) rightly described the attributions in our book as 'rather speculative' and some of them certainly were. Being a little foolhardy and sticking our necks out was important because so little written and comparative material survives in Ireland and until we

---

21   Michael McCarthy (ed.), *Lord Charlemont and His Circle*, Dublin, 2001

started to photograph nobody but Bodkin had. Strickland has no illustrations, except a few portraits of artists. Thomas Bodkin, who had left the National Gallery of Ireland to become the first Director of the Barber Institute in Birmingham, was the first to publish on Irish landscape and there are a number of illustrations in his book.[22] Going further back we found some useful sources though nearly all were based on Pasquin, who published his seminal and irreverent essay entitled *An Authentic History of the Artists of Ireland* in 1796. His followers were William Carey, W.B.S. Taylor, Warburton, Whitelaw and Walsh and the articles in some issues of the early nineteenth-century magazine *The Citizen* by 'M', who turned out to be the artist T.J. Mulvany.[23]

A contemporary source published since our first book is a highly important magazine which became a yearbook in 1988, *The Irish Arts Review*. It has been the repository of all Irish art historical research. Founded by Brian de Breffni and Anne Reihill, and after Brian's death edited by Alastair Smith, It is now being orchestrated by Homan Potterton, who had been director of the National Gallery of Ireland. Speculation sometimes let us down. For instance a fine signed and dated portrait of 1745 and two signed works seen in America by Desmond set us on the trail of Philip Hussey but it faded out and we made a hash of his later career. Two highly decorative conversation pieces one in the National Gallery of Ireland and the other in the Ulster Museum turned out to be by a Cumbrian artist Strickland Lowry. The most important reference in an inventory which identified one of the pictures as a Strickland Lowry was found by Eileen Black of the Ulster Museum, who had been one of Anne's students.

Anne's first post-graduate student was Jeanne Sheehy who in her interview said she wanted to do something on the French Impressionists. Anne was dubious as they had been so thoroughly worked over and suggested Walter Osborne whom Jeanne had hardly heard of but she said she would consider it and a few days later she took on

---

22 Thomas Bodkin, *Four Irish Landscape Painters*, Dublin and London, 1920
23 William Carey, *Some Memoirs of the Patronage and Progress of the Fine Arts in England and Ireland*, London, 1826; William B. Sarsfield Taylor, *The Origins, Progress and Present Condition of the Fine Arts in Great Britain and Ireland*, 2 Vols, London, 1841; J. Warburton, J. Whitelaw and R. Walsh, *History of the City of Dublin*, 2 Vols, London, 1818

Osborne with great enthusiasm. In the same year as the *Painters of Ireland* Jeanne contributed the nineteenth and twentieth centuries to a book entitled *Irish Art and Architecture* written with Homan Potterton, who dealt with 1600 - 1800, and Peter Harbison on pre-history to 1600. Homan's section was also an excellent summary. He too had been a student. Without the aid of Anne's post-graduate students like Jeanne, Julian Campbell and John Hutchinson, all of whom went on to curate exhibitions in the National Gallery which helped enormously as we had the opportunity of seeing a great many works and prevented our nineteenth-century chapters from being very lean. Roy Johnson wrote a thesis on Roderic O'Conor which was a great help and which he has used subsequently in exhibitions at Pont Aven. Jane Fenlon took over the seventeenth century, an apparently impossible task, and wrote her Ph.D. on the period's most famous Irish patrons, the Duke and Duchess of Ormonde, as well as the artists of the time. Subsequently she has enormously enlarged her knowledge and ours of all our seventeenth-century artists. More recently Toby Barnard of Hertford College Oxford shares with us his incredible archival researches into Irish life in the seventeenth and eighteenth centuries. Many others helped in smaller ways and our debt to them all is enormous as naturally we had jobs as well as book writing and had little enough time for research. Some of course are now important figures in the Irish scene of which we have room only to mention one, Peter Murray now the Curator in the Crawford Art Gallery in Cork who did a thesis with Anne on Petrie.

Along the way we collected a large corpus of drawings and watercolours and our next effort was a book *The Watercolours of Ireland*, published in 1994, also by Barrie and Jenkins. It had an American edition. By this time the large pastels by Hugh Douglas Hamilton had come to light, mostly executed in Italy, and it is a recognition of the stature of his work that his *Lord Guilford* hangs now in the National Gallery in Washington and his Tresham and Canova was bought by the Victoria and Albert Museum. His late Irish and Italian oils are also masterpieces, particularly his Earl

Bishop of Derry with his granddaughter in the Borghese gardens and, in striking contrast, the dramatic grief ridden portrait of Colonel Mansergh St. George, both now in the National Gallery of Ireland. In the meantime Fintan Cullen. a student from University College, Dublin had taken up the study of Hamilton's oils, which was published in the Walpole Society, Vol. L (1984). *Watercolours* gave us the opportunity to do justice to George Petrie, Sir Frederick William Burton, Andrew Nicholl and the ladies who founded the Watercolour Society, Fanny Curry and Harriet Keane to name but two. Also prominent in watercolour exhibitions in England and Ireland were Rose Barton, Mildred Anne Butler and Helen O'Hara. We both remember the unforgettable time of finding all the works of Mildred Anne Butler still in cupboards and under the stairs with notebooks, sketchbooks, cuttings etc. in total chaos at her old home in Kilmurry, County Kilkenny.

Watercolours was also interesting from a socio-historical point of view and we devoted a chapter to primitives and amateurs as they added a certain reality and zest to Ireland's pictorial past. We also devoted a chapter to the Irish in the colonies where we found the artistic training given to naval and army officers made them virtually professional artists. A good example is Robert Hood and his superb Canadian Arctic scenes and studies of birds. Glen Wilson though not in the service, did noble work in the South Pacific and the non-military engineer William Armstrong who gives such a wonderful view of young Canada, its railways, lakes and Indians. We could mention many more. In between we wrote articles which added tiny nuggets of new information and it then became obvious after *Watercolours* that we would have to return to painting to consolidate over 20 years of research since 1978 by ourselves and an increasing number of other workers in the field. In the new book to be published by Yale in the autumn of 2002 we speculate on newly discovered families of artists like the Pope Stevens, we discuss at some length the history of collecting in Ireland and bring the date of the book up to the mid-twentieth century. We have had the benefit of Hilary Pyle's work on Yeats and his family, of Gifford Lewis on Edith Somerville and the Yeats sisters and Kenneth McConkey on Lavery, Edwardian portraiture and many other topics. Then there are the two Brian Kennedys on the more modern period, one (an ex post-graduate student) now Keeper of Art in the Ulster Museum and whose recent book on Paul Henry is extremely interesting, and the other who is now the Director of the National Gallery of Australia in Canberra. Nicky Figgis (another ex-student) has written most of the Irish entries for Ingamell's *Dictionary of British and Irish Travellers in Italy 1701 - 1800* (1997) as she has specialised on the Irish in Rome a subject she tackles elsewhere in this catalogue. Theo Snoddy from Belfast has continued the work of Strickland into the twentieth century.

There are also now a number of very focused and extremely knowledgeable collectors of Irish art of all periods who have placed their pictures in some magnificently restored houses We must not forget the dealers particularly the late Cynthia O'Connor, as well as Christopher Foley in London and James and Therese Gorry in Dublin. Desmond has worked with Christie's during all these years and their help and that of Sotheby's was of enormous value to us. The doyennes of the Irish art market, Alan and Mary Hobart, who suggested that we should write this seemingly self-indulgent piece, have done so much to raise the profile of Irish art generally. This is their second catalogue of eighteenth-century Irish painting, a subject dear to our hearts, and in which they are internationally acknowledged as the leading dealers. They have brought together a wonderful array of paintings by familiar names such as Fagan, Roberts, Ashford and James Arthur O'Connor as well as lesser known, but equally, interesting artists such as John Lewis and Charles Collins, two figures about whom so much more has been discovered since we wrote the *Painters of Ireland*. We can feel proud to have aided and abetted in popularising our country's painters.

1.

Edward Luttrell
(circa 1650 – circa 1724)

A Pair of Portraits of a Lady and a Gentleman

Pastel on copper

14 x 11 ins

36 x 28 cms

Each signed and dated lower left 1698

Portrait of a Gentleman bears a label on verso inscribed: "Benjamin Bright found in… picture at Ham Green and…to…Museum from County"

Portrait of a Lady bears inscription: "Portraits the property of Wm (?) Sandby, Richmond, Surrey, Purchased at Sale by Auction on the demise of his widow 1819, painted by Luttrell on copper 1698"

Mystery surrounds the life of Edward Luttrell one of the earliest pioneers of the mezzotint technique. According to both Pilkington and Strickland, who may have been relying on sources since lost, he was born in Dublin in about 1650. It has, however, also been suggested that he was related to the Luttrell family of Saunton Court, Devon to which the famous diarist Narcissus Luttrell belonged.[24] He went to London as a young man and studied law at New Inn but abandoning this career he turned to art. According to Vertue he was self-taught but his technique suggests that he may have studied with Edmund Ashfield to whom he refers favourably in his manuscript treatise *An Epitome of Painting Containing Breife Directions for Drawing, Painting, Limning and Crayons…And how to Lay the Ground and Work in Mezzo Tinto,* which is dated 1683 and dedicated to his "much Honoured and most Ingenuous Kinswoman Dorothy Luttrell" (Yale Centre for British Art). In particular Ashfield's pastel of the 1st Duke of Ormonde, (National Gallery of Ireland) comes very close to Luttrell's slightly later work. Luttrell spent most of his life in London, living in Westminster where it seems

---

24 Patrick Noon, *English Portrait Drawings and Miniatures,* Yale, 1979, pp. 11 - 12

he had a shop selling prints. He was included in Vertue's list of "living painters of note in London" and in 1711 was appointed a director of Kneller's academy. Although Strickland and other sources give a date for his death as 1710 a dated work of 1724 seems to have survived.[25]

Eighteenth-century Ireland produced some of the greatest mezzotint artists of the day including James McArdell and Thomas Frye. Luttrell may be seen as their predecessor. As Strickland notes: "attracted to the newly-introduced art of mezzotint he endeavoured to obtain a knowledge of the process by bribing Blois, the workman who laid the grounds for Blooteling; but failing in this he began to experiment for himself with a view to obtaining the effects of Blooteling's prints. Eventually he made the acquaintance of J. van Somer who explained to him the process."[26] Most of his prints date from 1681 to 1710 and were engraved after his own drawings. They were among the earliest mezzotints by any English or Irish-born artist and bear witness to his slightly rudimentary understanding of the technique, lacking the supple refinement of say Frye's work. He also collaborated on several plates with Isaac Beckett.

Related to his mezzotints are works such as the present pair of portraits, showing a husband and wife. They are executed in what Anne Crookshank and the Knight of Glin characterise as the "eccentric medium" of pastel on copper.[27] Luttrell's *Portrait of a Man* in the National Gallery of Ireland dated to the following year, 1699, is in the same technique with the copper plate roughened as if for mezzotint but with pastel applied instead. The medium gives a certain glowing warmth to the pastel, clearly apparent in the present portraits. In his manuscript treatise referred to above Luttrell claims that he was the first artist to use this technique. This is supported by Walpole although William Faithorne has also been credited with the discovery. The portrait of the man in the present pair is closely related to a similar work by the artist which has been identified as showing Sir Christopher Wren.[28]

25 Ellis Waterhouse, *British 18th-Century Painters in Oils and Crayons*, Woodbridge, 1981, p. 228
26 Strickland, pp. 29 - 30
27 Crookshank / Glin, 1978, p. 71
28 Sold Sotheby's 22nd November 1979, lot 93

Figure 9 Henrietta Dering, *9 Portraits of Members of the Perceval Family*, (private collection)

Clearly interested in technical experimentation, as well as his works on copper Luttrell painted a pastel on an oak panel (National Portrait Gallery, London). In addition to portraits Luttrell produced many copies after Rembrandt. One of his most intriguing works, again executed in pastel on copper, shows five heads in imitation of the Dutch artist, which may be interpreted as depicting his family.[29] He also drew genre scenes such as *An Irish Sweep at the Crossing – Clarigis Street* (private collection) which is dated 1674 and inscribed in Latin as drawn from life. Perhaps his finest work, however, is a portrait of the Irish martyr St Oliver Plunkett and the other Catholic victims of the "Popish Plot", one of the great treasures of Stonyhurst College, which was seemingly drawn at Newgate Prison while Plunkett was awaiting execution.[30] Another drawing showing Plunkett alone is in the Bodleian Library, Oxford. Portraits of Plunkett circulated quite widely

---

29 *Rembrandt in Eighteenth-century England*, Exhibition Catalogue, Yale Centre for British Art, New Haven, 1983, no. 22
30 I am indebted to Fr Antony Symondson, S.J. for discussing this subject at length with me.

(if discretely) in the last decades of the seventeenth century with many versions known by Garret Morphey. Amongst these, however, the Stonyhurst work is unusual in clearly being a devotional image which would certainly seem to indicate that Luttrell was a Catholic. However he also drew Michael Hewetson the Anglican Archdeacon of Armagh and Gilbert Burnet, Bishop of Salisbury.

As Anne Crookshank and the Knight of Glin note Luttrell's pastels seem to have influenced Henrietta Dering, one of the finest Irish amateur artists of the period.[31] This is perhaps particularly apparent in her important group of nine portraits of members of the Perceval family (private collection) (figure 9). This can be dated to 1704 – 1705 a few years after the present pair of portraits. The similarities, though possibly generic, are indeed striking and may perhaps be seen as further evidence for Luttrell's Irish connections.[32]

(W.L.)

31 Anne Crookshank and the Knight of Glin, *Irish Portraits, 1660 – 1860*, London, 1969, p. 29
32 In 1708 Dering left for America settling in Charleston and is now claimed as one of the earliest American woman artists.

2.
Willem van der Hagen
(died 1745)

A Capriccio Landscape with Figures and Classical Ruins by a River

Oil on canvas

53 x 64 ins

135 x 163 cms

Provenance: Pallister House (later Loreto Abbey), Rathfarnham, County Dublin

Eighteenth-century Dublin saw one of the most innovative programmes of public building of any modern European city in which many émigré artists, most famously the Italian stucco workers, were involved. In addition to the famous public buildings many fine private mansions were constructed including Pallister House built in Rathfarnham outside Dublin for the son of the Archbishop of Cashel, William Pallister. The design of the house is reputedly by Edward Lovett Pearce, architect of the Parliament House although as with so many of Pearce's commissions no documentary evidence survives to support this attribution. Part of the original furnishings of Pallister House (later Loreto Abbey), the present landscape is a virtuoso display of van der Hagen's talents. Born in the Hague, he had arrived in Dublin in 1722 about three years before the construction of the house and the suave elegance of his style fitted perfectly with the sophisticated taste of early Georgian Ireland.

Before reaching Dublin, van der Hagen worked in the North of England painting topographical views in Yorkshire and Northamptonshire. From 1721 and 1722 date views of Gibraltar although (as with Ashford later) it is unlikely that he ever visited the Rock relying instead on engravings. The first record of van der Hagen in Ireland is in connection with his sets for the Theatre Royal.[33] Some years later in 1733 his

---

33 *Harding's Imperial Newsletter*, September 29th 1722; for a fuller account of van der Hagen's life particularly the question of the confusion surrounding the different members of the family see Crookshank / Glin / Laffan, pp. 14 - 19

scenery for Cephalus and Procris was praised as "finer painted than any ever seen in this kingdom".[34] The range and diversity of his work in Ireland surely belie Pasquin's unflattering assessment of his character.[35] In 1724 van der Hagen painted an altarpiece for St Michan's which has not survived nor has the "painted glory" for St Patrick's Church in Waterford. Four years later he was commissioned by the tapestry maker Robert Baillie to "take prospects" of the scenes to be depicted in the six tapestries for the newly built House of Lords. In the end only two of his paintings were worked up into tapestries and these depart from his designs considerably. For the Corporation of Waterford he painted a view of the city while views of Derry, Drogheda and the house and gardens of Carton are also known.

Van der Hagen was also active as a decorative artist painting "many houses in this kingdom".[36] His most elaborate recorded scheme was for the Beresford family at Curraghmore where he seems to have employed all the repertoire of a baroque illusionist. He painted an entire downstairs room with landscapes while the staircase was decorated with "columns, festoons etc between which are several landscapes". The ceiling was "painted in perspective and represents a Dome, the columns seeming to rise, though on a flat surface".[37] Also in County Waterford he decorated Whitfieldstown for the Christmas family.[38] This alone of van der Hagen's decorative schemes seems to have survived if, as seems likely, it is identical with the eighteen grisaille panels of classical divinities recently on the London art market. Similar designs were once to be found at Seafield Hall, Donabate, where feigned statues of classical figures appeared on six panels on two long walls of the saloon. Surprisingly given the refined elegance of his landscapes and capriccios and in particular their accomplished handling of architecture, the remaining fragments of van der Hagen's decorative

---

34 *Faulkner's Dublin Journal*, March 1733

35 "Had his industry been proportioned to his power, he might have done wonders; but he would never work while he had a shilling and, when pinched by his distresses, he would retire to a public house, and paint a picture to liquidate his reckoning." Pasquin, pp. 28 - 29

36 Liam Price (ed.), *An Eighteenth Century Antiquary, The Sketches, Notes and Diaries of Austin Cooper, 1759 – 1830*, Dublin, 1942, p. 181

37 Charles Smith, *The Ancient and Present State of the County and City of Waterford*, Dublin, 1746, p. 108

38 *Ibid.*, p. 97

schemes give a slightly unhappy impression. Clearly his forte lay elsewhere and it was to be in plaster not paint that the rococo burst upon Ireland during the artist's lifetime.

The present landscape has particular interest in the artist's oeuvre in that we can trace its early provenance to the fine Georgian mansion of Pallister House built by the son of the Archbishop of Cashel. Like many of the senior members of the Church of Ireland Archbishop Pallister was English, the family originally coming from Yorkshire. He entered Trinity College Dublin at the age of fourteen, becoming a fellow in 1668. He enjoyed swift preferment in the Church being appointed Bishop of Colyne in 1692 and Archbishop of Cashel two years later. These appointments brought great wealth which was consolidated by the marriage of his son William to the Accountant General for Ireland. It was William Pallister who on the death of his father constructed the house and who, presumably therefore, was van der Hagen's patron. Clearly a man of taste and learning his memory is preserved in the Bibliotheca Pallisteriana which he bequeathed to the library of Trinity College. Among the other treasures of Pallister House was a remarkable saloon hung with early eighteenth century gilt leather.[39] In 1821 Mother Teresa established her convent of Loreto Abbey at the House and until recently it was home to a leading Dublin School.

The Pallister House Capriccio shows a river scene with magnificent classical architecture falling into decay and contrasting sharply with the humble activities of the staffage. A fisherman casts a long line into the river while beggars pause at the foot of the row of corinthian columns. Further into the distance small boats come to shore and around the large house on the far bank, with washing hanging from its central window, figures and horses go about their daily life. Dominating the right bank of the river looms a fortress, its central tower not dissimilar to the Castel Sant'Angelo in Rome but surrounded by imposing defensive fortifications. One slightly puzzling element of the scene is the pair of orientalised figures conversing in the shadows cast by the

39 See John Cornforth, "Aglow with Golden Leather", in *County Life*, November 26th 1987, pp. 61 - 63

Figure 10 Willem van der Hagen, *A River Landscape,* private collection

architecture in the foreground. Van der Hagen applies the paint smoothly with great delicacy of touch. The composition is unified by the confident handling of the perspective and the related tones of his palette

The present landscape seems to be one of the earliest in date of van der Hagen's remarkable series of capriccio landscapes. A date of about 1730 would fit with the little we know of the construction history of Pallister House. A smaller variant of it survives (figure 10) which closely replicates most of the composition, with the main difference being the lack of the prominent columns on the left hand side. This is dated 1732 and has all the hallmarks of a later variant by the artist on a more commercial scale, perhaps painted for the open market rather than on commission. Indeed it is from the

Figure 11 Willem van der Hagen, *Figures and Animals with Classical Ruins*, reproduction courtesy of the National Gallery of Ireland

early 1730s that the majority of van der Hagen's capriccios seem to date. Also from 1732 is the small work in the National Gallery of Ireland in which the treatment of the architecture covered with vegetation is extremely similar (figure 11). Different elements predominate in van der Hagen's capriccios of the 1730s showing the various influences which the artist draws on to produce these highly distinctive works. In paintings such as the present example there is an emphasis on classical architecture with a strong sense of perspective recalling in ways the stage designs of the Bibiena family. A related but quite separate group are the so-called Southern Harbours (see figure 12) which include large scale shipping at port and usually a greater bustle of figures. Ultimately derived from Claude's works such as *The Embarkation of the Queen of Sheba* (National Gallery, London), a more immediate influence may have been Weenix's works of identical subject matter which van der Hagen may have seen in his native Netherlands and certainly in English collections. While a chronology is difficult to establish it is tempting to suggest that later in the 1730s van der Hagen turned more towards pure landscape. In the important work formerly in Kilsharvan House and dated 1736 the ruins take a

Figure 12 Willem van der Hagen, *A Southern Harbour*, private collection

Figure 13 Willem van der Hagen, *A Capriccio Landscape with Shepherds*, private collection,

much lesser role while the rather Arcadian landscape predominates (figure 13).[40] Interestingly the last record of the artist in 1745 is in connection with a print by John Brooks after his view of the Powerscourt Waterfall suggesting that by this date he was beginning to work in the direction of the picturesque taken up a decade or so later by artists such as Barret and Forrester.

The importance of van der Hagen's example to the creation of the great landscape school that flourished in Ireland in the second half of the century simply cannot be overstated. In the finest of his capriccio landscapes van der Hagen equals the achievement of his contemporaries in Europe, indeed often anticipating developments on the continent. An example will illustrate this. On his grand tour Joseph Leeson, 1st Earl of Milltown purchased a set of capriccio landscapes from the acknowledged master of the genre Giovanni Paolo Panini (National Gallery of Ireland). These are dated 1742, at least ten years after the present work. A comparison with one (figure 14) demonstrates similarities in handling of the architectural motifs and placement of the figure groups. While a comparison is invidious it is reasonable to suggest that Leeson could have acquired as good a capriccio back in Dublin. However, the lure of the Italian was always a strong element in the purchasing decisions of the Irish aristocracy. Later in

---

40 See Crookshank / Glin / Laffan, pp. 14 - 19

the century Robert Carver (see catalogue 7) complained: "I have some pieces at home which would be no disgrace to a gentleman's dining-room, but they would be known to be mine, and no one would vouchsafe to look upon the paltry daubings…[but if I] gave it out that they were executed by Signor Sombodini, all the connoisseurs in town would flock about them".[41] Until recently, it may be argued, a similar attitude has prevailed with the work of Irish artists, both native and resident, being unfairly denigrated in comparison to painting by artists of the great centres of London and the continent. Now just as architects such as Pearce are being acknowledged as among the most original of the period, artists such as van der Hagen working in the cosmopolitan milieu of Dublin in the first half of the eighteenth century must be hailed as the equal of their continental counterparts.

(A.O.C. & K. of G.)

---

41 J.T. Gilbert, *A History of the City of Dublin*, Dublin, 1859, Vol. III, pp. 347 – 48. One cannot help feeling that this outburst may have been prompted by the recent success in Dublin of the Italian landscape painter Gabrielli Ricciardelli.

Figure 14 Giovanni Paolo Panini, *A Capriccio with the Forum*,
          reproduction courtesy of the National Gallery of Ireland

3.

Charles Collins

(circa 1700 – 1744)

A Still Life with Game

Oil on canvas

38 ¼ x 44 ins

97 x 112 cms

Signed and dated lower left: "C. Collins 1741"

One of the most significant Irish artists to have emerged since the publication of Anne Crookshank and the Knight of Glin's *The Painters of Ireland* is the still life painter Charles Collins. Although mentioned by Strickland he had fallen into obscurity and in 1981 when his striking *Still Life with a Lobster on a Delft Dish* (figure 15) was purchased by the Tate Gallery the little that was known of his life was hopelessly confused. His dates were routinely wrongly stated and his connections with Ireland blurred. A review of the evidence, however, reveals Collins to have been one of the most accomplished painters working in Ireland in the first half of the eighteenth century.

Since Sir William Gilbey's important work *Animal Painters of England from 1650* the date of Collins' birth has usually been given as 1680.[42] This is implausible. Vertue in noting his death in 1744 states that the artist was then aged between 40 and 50.[43] Supporting evidence for a birth date of around 1700 comes from the paintings themselves. His earliest known work is dated 1729 and after this a sequence of dated oils and watercolours can be established for most years until his death. Accepting the earlier date for his birth would rather improbably suppose no work had survived until the artist was aged almost fifty. At the same time there is explicit early evidence for Collins' Irish nationality. He is specifically referred to as an "Irish Master" in the *Dublin*

---

42 Sir William Gilbey, *Animal Painters of England from 1650*, London, 1900, Vol. 1, pp. 102 - 3

43 George Vertue, "The Notebooks of George Vertue Relating to Artists and Collections in England", Vol. 3, *Walpole Society*, Vol. XXII, 1933 - 34, p. 122

Figure 15 Charles Collins, *Still Life with a Lobster on a Delft Dish*, ©Tate, London, 2001

Evening Post of 4th May 1786. This is in the context of the sale of the collection of the doctor and property developer Gustavus Hume in which a painting of the same subject as the present work is favourably noted: "a dead hare, dead birds etc…allowed by the first judges in point of elegance and performance, to be inferior to none".[44] Seemingly this formed a pendant to another work by the artist showing live fowl. It is further to be noted that a still life by Collins was included in the collection of James Digges La Touche sold in Geminiani's rooms in Dublin in May 1764.[45] The presence

44 *Dublin Evening Post*, 4th May 1786
45 *A Catalogue of the genuine collection of Italian, Flemish and other Pictures of the Late James Digges Latouche, Esq. Deceased, Dublin, 16th May 1764*

of Collins' work in two Dublin collections within a few years of his death strongly supports the explicit statement of the *Dublin Evening Post* as to Collins' nationality.

Collins worked in both oil and watercolour and seems to have been almost exclusively a painter of still lifes. Vertue refers to him as a "bird painter" (although also noting a self portrait) Walpole as a painter of "all sorts of fowl and game".[46] Together with Peter Paillou he worked on watercolours of British birds and mammals for the collector Taylor White.[47] These large sheets have long been admired. Perhaps the greatest connoisseur of English watercolours, Iolo Williams, recounts an amusing anecdote. "One of my most exciting experiences as a collector…was when, one day in, I suppose, 1931 my wife and I got off a bus in the Brompton Road and saw the windows of Parson's shop (now alas no longer there) filled entirely with birds by Collins. It was then the worst moment of the slump and the drawings were marked at what even then were fantastically low prices – either £1 1s and £1 10s or 15s and £1 1s each, I forget which. Even at these prices the family finances at that moment would not allow me to buy more than two – but I have never got better value or more pleasure for about 30s. In two or three days the whole lot was gone."[48]

The Taylor White collection was sold at Sotheby's on 6th June 1926 and some two hundred watercolours from it are now preserved at McGill University, Montreal. Collins seems to have worked on these watercolours from the mid-1730s until his death. Some were engraved for ornithological works such as those by Henry Fletcher and James Mynde and it has been suggested that in them he was influenced by the sixteenth-century Bolognese naturalist Ulisi Aldrovandi.[49] Jane Fenlon has further observed a direct connection between two watercolours (one depicting a heron (1737) and another a bittern (1735)) and Paul de Vos' *Wading Birds in a Landscape*.[50] The

---

46 Vertue, *op. cit.*, for Walpole see Strickland, Vol. 1, p. 188
47 See Christine E. Jackson, *Bird Painting in the Eighteenth Century*, Woodbridge, 1994, p. 50
48 Iolo A. Williams, *Early English Watercolours and some Cognate Drawings by Artists born not Later than 1785*, London, 1952, (1970), p. 27
49 John Murdoch, *Forty British Watercolours from the Victoria and Albert Museum*, London, 1977, no. 1
50 See Anne Crookshank and the Knight of Glin, *The Watercolours of Ireland*, London, 1994, p. 109 and n. 5

Figure 16 Charles Collins, *A Landscape with British Birds*, Anglesey Abbey,
The Fairhaven Collection (The National Trust).
Photograph: Photographic Survey, Courtauld Institute of Art

drawings show exceptional skill at the rendering of plumage and the characterization of the individual birds fully justifying Williams' description of Collins as the finest English bird painter.[51]

Collins' oils display many of the same characteristics as this series of watercolours. Of particular note is a series of twelve large canvases of British birds, nine of which are now owned by the National Trust at Anglesea Abbey (figure 16). Dated 1736 and engraved in the same year, they show a total of 115 birds from 58 species all set in beautifully rendered landscapes.[52] Painted five years later the present work is one of

---

51 Williams, *op. cit.* p. 27
52 There is an intriguingly close parallel between these bird pictures and an engraving showing birds of different species similarly scattered in Robert Dodsley, "Of Drawing", *The Preceptor*, Dublin, 1748, which was to be a key element of the teaching of the Dublin Society Schools.

Figure 17 Charles Collins, *Still Life with a Hunting Dog and Dead Game*, private collection

a group of still lifes of dead game most of which date, like the watercolours, from the last decade of Collins' life. Set on a ledge in a wooded landscape are shown a hare, a mallard and a partridge surrounding a hunting gun and powder flask. Small pellets of shot spill out onto the ground showing how the animals met their fate while further birds circle nervously in the sky as if the hunt is still continuing. In the distance a mansion nestles at the foot of a distinctive rocky crag. The landscape seems topographical rather than imaginary. Its identification would be an important clue to a further understanding of Collins' career.

As in earlier Dutch still life painting the seemingly casual display of game is in fact quite artful. The composition is elegantly arranged around the diagonal of the gun crossing the strong central vertical of the hanging hare. The extensive vista to the right contrasts with the busy foreground and shows Collins' ability as a landscape artist. The great charm of the picture, however, which is emphasised by the work's fine state of preservation, is the highly polished paint surface and the treatment of the still life group. Collins takes evident joy in differentiating between the different textures of the fur and the plumage of the animals. The fur of the hare shows an almost *trompe l'oeil* illusionism. This quality was noted by Williams: "occasionally Collins painted dead birds as an exercise in sheer virtuosity in the rendering of feathers".[53] The many hundreds of zoological watercolours that he executed, seemingly from life, clearly gave the artist a great insight into the anatomy of game. Many of the same elements are apparent in a related work (figure 17) in which the composition is expanded horizontally, the axis of the gun is reversed and the landscape replaced by rather incongruous formal gardens.

The genre of hunting still lifes, popular throughout the seventeenth and eighteenth centuries, seems first to have been employed by Frans Snyders in about 1610. It was refined by his followers such as Jan Fyt who was the first to set the still life in a landscape background and include hunting paraphernalia. Two French contemporaries of Collins, Alexandre-François Desportes and Jean-Baptiste Oudry continued the tradition adding new variants to the formula. However, the artist whose hunting still lifes most clearly seem to have influenced him is Jan Weenix. Weenix was immensely successful in this genre and many of the motifs which Collins deploys are first seen in his work. He was particularly popular in England where his work was collected within his own lifetime and it is certain that Collins could have seen examples in English and possibly Irish collections. However, given his deep understanding of its art it is tempting to hypothesise a trip by Collins to the Low Countries. This would neatly explain the almost complete absence of mention of him by contemporary

---

53 Williams, *op. cit.*, p. 27

writers on art and could be paralleled by the example of William Gowe Ferguson, a slightly earlier Scottish painter of still lifes who worked mostly in the Netherlands.

The Irish aristocracy of the eighteenth century was often mocked by English visitors for living only for the pleasures of the table and the hunt. While we do not know for certain that the present still life

Figure 18 Robert Hunter, *Peter La Touche of Bellevue*, reproduction courtesy of the National Gallery of Ireland

was painted in Ireland it may be best viewed as a reflection of this culture. As do so many game still lifes, it revels in the physicality of the spoils of the hunt. We noted above that a painting of a pheasant by Collins was in the Dublin collection of James Digges La Touche sold in 1764. Shortly after this his kinsman, Peter La Touche was painted by Robert Hunter in a portrait (National Gallery of Ireland) which comes close in spirit to Collins' game still lifes (figure 18). La Touche is shown reclining in a landscape cradling his gun and stroking his dog with a brace of game birds at his side. In the Netherlands of the seventeenth century where the game still life first arose as an independent genre, hunting was strictly regulated by class. Certain animals and birds were reserved for the aristocracy, and the wealthy bourgeoisie were forbidden to hunt them even on their own estates. It has been suggested that the rise of the game still life may have, in part, derived from an attempt on the part of the new middle

Figure 19 Sir William Orpen, *Study for The Dead Ptarmigan*, Pyms Gallery

classes to ape the taste of the aristocracy.[54] A similar pattern may be suggested for Ireland using the example of the La Touches.[55] The founder of the dynasty arrived in Ireland in 1671 an immigrant from the religious turmoil in France. They quickly became the leading bankers and merchants of Dublin and were to go on to found the Bank of Ireland. By the second generation they were among the richest families in Ireland but still lacked a title. Nevertheless the Hunter portrait pretends to a certain aristocratic languor. The game still life they bought from Collins may well have been a similar means of identifying the family with the pursuits of the Irish aristocracy.

Collins is without doubt the greatest still life painter to have worked in Ireland in the eighteenth century. Indeed he had little competition in the genre apart from the occasional stiff flower piece by Ashford and the paintings of Charles Lewis who worked in Dublin in the 1770s and 80s and whose still lifes of fruit seem to owe something to Collins' pictures of the same subject. Indeed it was not for some hundred and fifty years that his achievement in the depiction of dead game was equalled in Irish art by Orpen's masterly *Study for The Dead Ptarmigan* (figure 19).

(W.L.)

---

54 See Seymour Slive, *Dutch Painting*, 1600 – 1800, Yale, 1995, p. 288 - 89
55 For the family see most recently Sergio Benedetti, *The La Touche Amorino*, National Gallery of Ireland, Dublin, 1998

4.

John Lewis
(circa 1720 – 1776)

A Classical Landscape with the Story of Cimon and Iphigenia

27 x 41 ¾ ins

68.5 x 106 cms

signed and dated lower right "J. Lewis 1758"

Literature: William Laffan, "'Taste, Elegance and Execution', John Lewis as a
Landscape Painter" in *Irish Arts Review Yearbook*, Vol. 15, 1999, pp. 151 – 53,
illustrated in colour, fig. 1

John Lewis' oeuvre is largely in the process of being rediscovered and he is emerging as one of the most interesting artists working in Dublin in the middle of the eighteenth century. The present work is the finest of his handful of known landscapes. Like van der Hagen (see catalogue 2) and Robert Carver (see catalogue 7) Lewis worked as a scene painter in the Dublin theatres as well as painting portraits and landscapes. Details of his life are sketchy. He may have been English, or perhaps Welsh, and was the brother-in-law of Stephen Slaughter who visited Dublin for the first time in or about 1734.[56] Early works of Lewis, which may well have been executed in Ireland, include *The Judgement of Midas* (private collection) and *The Boy in Blue* (private collection). In 1750 Lewis began his highly successful association with Smock Alley Theatre, which coincided with the directorship of Thomas Sheridan whom Lewis painted and who became a close friend. His stage designs were radically different from anything seen previously in Dublin, redecorating the theatre "in a new taste" described at the time as being of such quality that "in point of taste, elegance of design and masterly execution [it] is allowed by the connoisseurs not to be inferior to any in Europe".[57]

Lewis painted many portraits of theatrical figures of which the most famous is his

---

56 Lewis married Slaughter's sister, Judith.
57 *Faulkner's Dublin Journal*, 11th – 15th October 1757

Portrait of Peg Woffington (National Gallery of Ireland) which survives in at least three versions. He also decorated Sheridan's house at Quilca, County Cavan, painting the ceilings and walls of the parlour "with sky and cloud scenery". Below were four portraits "one on each wall in large medallions of Milton, Shakespeare, Swift and old Dr Sheridan. These were supported by allegorical figures and set off by draperies and a goodly sized sphinx or two for the corners".[58] This description rather echoes the written account of the decorative scheme which van der Hagen executed at Curraghmore. Lewis left the employment of Smock Alley at the end of Sheridan's tenure but it seems likely that he stayed in Ireland for some period as he painted ten members of the Dobbyn family of County Waterford in 1759. As well as painting the theatrical world and provincial merchants such as the Dobbyns on at least one occasion Lewis received a commission from the Irish aristocracy as his fine portrait of Lady Moira (private collection) attests.

Lewis next emerges in London when, in 1762, he exhibited two portraits at the Society of Artists sending landscapes and still lifes to further exhibitions until 1776. The previous year he had been elected a director of the society. A series of large topographical works of country houses in the West of England survive which give bird's-eye views of the Devon countryside. It had previously been assumed that these were the work of another artist of the same name but detailed examination has established that the stylistic differences with the present work are superficial and caused by the different requirements of topographical and ideal landscape.[59] On the basis of these it has proved possible to tentatively attribute to Lewis a group of landscapes of the Enniskillen area at Florence Court, County Fermanagh showing that he may also have painted topographical views in Ireland. Lewis' work is varied. While some of the early portraits appear rather wooden, the *Portrait of Peg Woffington* is a fine, elegant image which perfectly captures the allure of its famous sitter. It was clearly a popular work as various versions of it are known and it inspired Roger

---

58 "B", "A Pilgrimage to Quilca in the Year 1852 with Some Accounts of the Old Belongings of the Place" in *Dublin University Magazine*, Vol. XL, Nov. 1852, p. 513

59 Waterhouse, for example, includes separate entries for the scene painter and the topographical artist; Ellis Waterhouse, *British 18th Century Painters in Oils and Crayons*, Woodbridge, 1981, pp. 222 – 23

O'More's "verses to be placed under the picture of the celebrated Mrs Woffington".[60]

Figure 20 Angelica Kauffman, *Cimon and Iphigenia*, private collection, formerly with Rafael Vals Ltd

The *Landscape with the Story of Cimon and Iphigenia* dates from 1758, the year after Lewis had left Smock Alley. It is likely that it was painted in Ireland and indeed elements of the scenery are typically Irish. Naturally, given his experience as a scene painter, Lewis was a talented landscape artist and in his earliest known work, *The Judgement of Midas*, while the mythological figures are rather clumsy, the landscape setting is much more accomplished. The present work is an altogether finer picture "painted with great panache suggestive of a scene painter's hand."[61] and seems to show the influence of Zuccarelli who had been working in England since 1752. As Anne Crookshank and the Knight of Glin note "the figures have an almost flickering, rococo liveliness".[62] Lewis can be seen to be on a similar path to the young Barret whose *Classical Landscape* (private collection) of 1755 compares closely in terms of palette. The group of figures are set in an open landscape which combines elements from the classical tradition (the ruin on the crag at upper left is clearly derived from the famous Roman remains on the Via Nomentana) with what appears to be the ruins of a gothic castle linked by a bridge to a further cluster of buildings which includes a church. In the middle distance a herd of cattle are being driven down to the river while on the far horizon a town is summarily indicated.

The subject of the landscape is Cimon and Iphigenia from Boccacio's *Decameron* in which Cimon, the son of a nobleman but living as a peasant happens upon a sleeping nymph

60 *Dublin Universal Advertiser*, 8th September 1753
61 William Laffan, "'Taste, Elegance and Execution', John Lewis as a Landscape Painter" in *Irish Arts Review Yearbook*, Vol. 15, 1999, p 153
62 Anne Crookshank and the Knight of Glin, *Irish Painting, 1600 – 1940*, (forthcoming 2002)

and suddenly has his mind opened to higher things and, by the contemplation of her beauty, becomes recivilised.[63] The story was translated by Dryden in 1700 and elements of the picture may suggest the artist's knowledge of this translation. Iphigenia is described as wearing "a purple vest" and Cimon as "leaning on his staff". Quite what prompted Lewis to paint this relatively obscure subject remains unclear. It may be noted, however, that ten years later in 1767 Garrick put on a version of the story in London and interestingly George Mullins exhibited a picture of the same

Figure 21 John Lewis, *Figures by a Natural Arch*, private collection

subject at the Society of Artists in Ireland in the same year.[64] Some years later Angelica Kauffman (who worked briefly in Ireland) painted the same subject and the rendering of the central group is rather close to Lewis' but reversed (figure 20).[65]

Two years ago the present author, writing of the rediscovery of *Cimon and Iphigenia* expressed the hope that it would lead "to the reattribution of other landscapes to Lewis and to his recognition as an important figure in the rise of the eighteenth-century landscape school in Ireland".[66] Happily, this has indeed proved to be the case. A landscape showing elegant figures by a natural arch (figure 21) formerly tentatively given to Carver, is in fact clearly by Lewis. The palette is extremely close while the cloud formation is rendered almost identically. It is, however, a rather weaker picture, in particular the figures are awkwardly insubstantial, suggesting a slightly earlier date, perhaps about 1750.

(W.L.)

---

63 I am grateful to Elizabeth McGrath of the Warburg Institute for identifying the subject.
64 George Breeze, *Society of Artists in Ireland, Index of Exhibits, 1765 – 1780*, Dublin, 1985, p. 19
65 Lady V. Manners and Dr G. Williamson, *Angelica Kauffman, Her Life and Works*, London, 1924, pp. 180 and 235
66 Laffan, *op. cit.*, p. 153

James Forrester (1730 - 1776)
(catalogue 5 – 6)

Born in Dublin in July 1730, Forrester, a Roman Catholic, first attended the Dublin Society Schools under Robert West at the age of seventeen. In the mid-eighteenth century, as a pupil of the Schools, he would have been trained to compose landscapes by copying engravings after ideal, classical views of Claude Lorrain (1600 - 82) and Gaspard Dughet (1615 - 75). Showing talent, the young artist was awarded premiums by the Society in the years 1747 and 1750 and received first prize for drawing in 1751.

In 1755 Forrester moved to Rome, where he clearly enjoyed the company of other artists. The English landscape painter, Jonathan Skelton (circa 1735 - 1759), recorded on 20 August 1758:

> We have at Rome some very good young men among them students from Great Britain and Ireland. One of them is my very particular Friend, his name is Forrester, I have learn'd many excellent things from him in private Life. He studies Painting in my own way and is very ingenious.[67]

During his early years in the city, Forrester shared lodgings with the Irish artists Robert Crone (circa 1718 - 79) and Jacob Ennis (1728 - 70) on the Strada della Croce. In 1758 he lived in the same house near the Piazza di Spagna as Carlo Mariotti, an Italian history painter, and the French artist Louis Gabriel Blanchet (1705 - 72). By 1763 he had moved to the Strada Felice with the English architect, George Dance (1741 - 1825) and the amateur artist Peter Stephens. He is also recorded from 1765 to 1770, as residing with the English sculptor, Joseph Nollekens (1737 - 1823) on the Corso (No. 28).[68] Another close friend was the American artist, Benjamin West (1738 - 1820) who visited Italy from 1760 to 1763. From him Forrester received the technical secret on

---

67 Brinsley Ford (ed.), 'The Letters of Jonathan Skelton ...', *Walpole Society*, 1956 - 58, Vol. XXXVI, p. 58
68 Letter from Didier Bodart, dated 13th April 1974, I am grateful to Evelyne Bell for this information.

how to prepare "Jews Pitch" for his paintings.[69] He was also acquainted with Joseph Wright of Derby (1734 - 97), by then considered the English master of the 'candle-light' style, who mentions Forrester in the journal which he kept while in Italy from 1774 to 1775.[70]

In the hot summer months, Forrester would have been typical of the landscape painters, who made sketching expeditions to the Alban Hills, the foothills of which are only 12 km south of Rome. Such visits would have provided material for paintings like his *Italianate Landscape with Figures by a Tomb* painted in the 1770s (National Gallery of Ireland) as well as his contributions to Peter Stephens' *150 Views of Italy* published in 1767.[71]

Forrester also explored other parts of the Papal States, mostly in the area of present day Umbria. From 11th to 29th June 1769, he made an excursion with his artist friends George Robertson (1749 - 88), Nollekens and others, and they visited Bassano, Caprarola, Narni, Terni, Foligno, Spoleto, Loreto, Ancona, Seravalle, Macerata, Valcimara, Assisi and Perugia. Forrester kept a detailed daily record of the sites visited, which was published in 1787 by Robertson as *A Tour Made in Italy in the Year 1769*. In 1769 John Dawson, 1st Earl of Portarlington (who was also a friend and patron of Jonathan Fisher) purchased eight drawings of Italian scenes, which may well have been sketched on this trip.

In Rome, like other Irish landscape painters, including Solomon Delane (circa 1727 - 1812) and Crone, Forrester established a high reputation for his work, such as his *View of the Ponte Sisto*, which in 1771 he sent to the Royal Academy exhibition in London.[72] Generally Forrester continued to work in the manner of his early training, by

69 'Miscellaneous observations useful to Painters', published by George Robertson in *A Tour made in Italy in 1769*, p. 68. Transcript at Paul Mellon Centre for Studies in British Art, the Brinsley Ford Archive, London.
70 Brinsley Ford, *op. cit.*, p. 58
71 As well as contributing two drawings to this volume, he etched drawings after Stephens. See loose etchings, British Museum, Department of Prints and Drawings, C3*.
72 Sold Sotheby's, Florence, 25th May 1988 (lot 832)

producing views, elevated by the inclusion of classical ruins. Amongst his clients were John Stuart, 3rd Earl of Bute and William Petty, 2nd Earl Shelburne.

Forrester's most important patron, however, was the Jesuit-educated Henry Belling, 8th Baron Arundell of Wardour (1740 - 1808), who provided him with an annuity, which is probably the reason he was able to live on the Corso, a relatively expensive part of the city.[73] Together, the artist and Father John Thorpe, a former Jesuit priest, purchased old master paintings for Lord Arundell to add to his collection. Forrester took responsibility for the pictures before they were exported and consulted Thorpe as to cleaning and framing.[74] Alluding to the suppression of the Jesuits in 1773, Thorpe wrote to Lord Arundell:

> I have many & great obligations to Forrester who has laid by every other
> work to Serve me in your commissions, & in the present circumstances of
> the Jesuits in Rome I should have been hindered from serving you if I could
> not have had his honest assistance with assurance of secrecy.[75]

The register of deaths for the parish of S. Maria del Popolo records on 1st February 1776 that Forrester, aged 45, had died the previous evening.[76] A memorial to him in the Church of S. Maria del Popolo was recorded in 1869.[77]

73 Ingamells p. 371; letter from Father John Thorpe, 14th April 1776
74 *Ibid.*, p. 939
75 *Ibid.*, p. 371
76 Rome, S. Giovanni in Laterano, Archivio del Vicariato, *Liber Mortuorum*, S. Maria del Popolo, Vol. XII, f. 121
77 V. Forcella, *Iscrizioni delle Chiese e D'Altri Edifici di Roma*, Rome, 1869, Vol. I, p. 396, no. 1512. It was inscribed: "*Pictor. Amoenioris. Picturae, Argutiis. Clarus*".

5.

James Forrester

(circa 1730 – 1776)

The Fitzwilliam Forresters

A Pair of Landscapes

5A *Landscape with Monks by Lake Nemi*

5B *Figures by a Torrent in a Stormy Wooded Landscape*

Oil on canvas

52 x 76 ½ ins

132 x 194 cms

Signed and dated on a label attached to the stretcher:

"James Forrester / Pinxt Romae / 1766"

Provenance: 4th Earl Fitzwilliam, Milton House,

acquired in Rome in 1767

Thence by descent until after the Second World War

Literature: Brinsley Ford (ed.), 'The Letters of Jonathan Skelton ...',

Walpole Society, 1956 - 58, Vol. XXXVI, p. 58

Anne Crookshank and the Knight of Glin, *The Painters of Ireland,*

circa 1660 – 1920, London, 1978, p. 126

Gaspard Dughet a French Landscape Painter in 17th Century Rome

and his Influence on British Art, Exhibition Catalogue,

Kenwood House, London, 1980, p. 87

Ellis Waterhouse, *British 18th-Century Painters*, Woodbridge, 1981, p. 129

Nicola Figgis, 'Irish Landscapists in Rome 1750 - 1780',

Irish Arts Review, Vol. 4, No. 4, Winter 1987, p. 63

John Ingamells (ed.), *A Dictionary of British and Irish Travellers in Italy*

1701 - 1800, New Haven and London, 1997, pp. 361, 371

The fascination with nocturnal scenes and the effects of illumination originated with the work of Caravaggio. From the 1760s it suited the more Romantic style of landscape painting, largely inspired by Edmund Burke's treatise, *A philosophical inquiry into the origin of our ideas of the Sublime and the Beautiful* (London, 1757). Perhaps it is no coincidence that in 1766, the year in which Forrester executed these two paintings, the Irish artist, James Barry (1741 - 1806), an advocate of Burke's aesthetic theories, arrived in Rome. The interest in the sublime can be seen in paintings of storms, where man was seen powerless against the forces of nature; by contrast, beauty is shown in paintings of calm, serene scenes.

Moonlit scenes were a speciality of Forrester and were acquired by Lord Arundell of Wardour (1771) and William Henry, Duke of Gloucester, third son of Frederick, Prince of Wales. In 1767 while on his Grand Tour, William Wentworth Fitzwilliam, 2nd Earl Fitzwilliam (1748 - 1833),[78] purchased these two moonlight landscapes, one showing a calm night, the other showing stormy conditions, with which he was 'well pleased'.[79]

Lord Fitzwilliam, nephew and heir of Charles Wentworth, Marquis of Rockingham, had been educated at Eton and King's College, Cambridge. Accompanying him was his tutor the Reverend Thomas Crofts, who had been recommended by the Headmaster of Eton.[80] From 1764 to 1766 they travelled in France and Switzerland and arrived in Italy in 1767, where they spent a year. Apart from purchasing the two landscapes by Forrester, Fitzwilliam also acquired portraits by Titian and Federico Barocci. Fitzwilliam was an enthusiastic student of antiquity, writing to his mother of the ancient Roman ruins, that 'the elegance of their architecture, and the beauty of their sculpture surpass everything, that one sees of modern date'.[81]

Like most young men on their Grand Tour, Fitzwilliam's sojourn in Italy was not

---

78 In 1795 Fitzwilliam was appointed Lord Lieutenant of Ireland but was recalled after three months for showing sympathy with the demand for Catholic Emancipation.
79 Ingamells, p. 361
80 *Ibid.*
81 *Ibid.*

completely devoted to academic pursuits. In Florence he met his friends from Eton, Charles James Fox and the 5th Earl of Carlisle. According to Lord Kildare, who was also there, Fox was in love with a lady who had instead 'fixed her eye upon Fitzwilliam'.[82] In Rome he is said to have acquired at least two mistresses. On his return to England, in 1770 Fitzwilliam married Lady Charlotte Ponsonby (d. 1822), daughter of the 2nd Earl of Bessborough. After her death, his second marriage was to the Hon. Louisa Molesworth, daughter of the 3rd Viscount Molesworth and widow of the 1st Baron Ponsonby.

5A *Landscape with Monks by Lake Nemi*

In the past this prospect has been identified as overlooking Lake Albano. However, it is here given as Lake Nemi due to the inclusion of the Capuchin monks, whose monastery was situated at Genzano, overlooking this lake. In antiquity Lake Nemi was dedicated to the cult of Diana and a grove on the north east became one of the most celebrated sanctuaries in central Italy. In the late 4th Century B.C. the Temple of Diana Nemorensis was built there, in a position overlooking the lake, which would seem to be the ruined temple, featuring prominently on the right hand side of this painting.

The scene is set in the darkness of the night (which conveys a sense of the unknown) but there is a stillness and spirituality about this work, which contrasts with its companion painting. An opening in the clouds reveals the beauty of the full moon, which casts a reflection on the lake and provides a contrast to the darkness. The full moon signifies spiritual power and is also an allusion to Diana, the goddess of the moon.

In typically Claudian manner, the landscape is framed in the foreground by dominating elements on either side and the background recedes into distant hills. On the right is

---

82 *Ibid.*

the Temple, to the left a wooded area with several large trees in the foreground. The middle ground is occupied by Lake Nemi and rising from the opposite shore the woodland continues, interrupted to the left of centre by a classical building with an elaborate portico.

In the foreground, by the light of the moon, two Capuchin monks are seen, each in their private world. The one in the centre facing the lake, appears to kneel; the other, hooded and in greater obscurity, stands in prayer near a flat rock. To the right of the figures, four deer, associated with Diana, add to the natural beauty and tranquillity of the scene. In antiquity, by contrast, this was a place of sacrifice and savage ritual. To become a priest of Diana, a branch ('the golden bough') had to be broken off a particular tree in the grove by a runaway slave, who then had to kill the existing priest in single combat.[83] The branch seen lying on the ground in front of the temple near to the deer may be a reference to the golden bough.

This work shows Forrester's consummate skill in painting nocturnal subjects. The moon itself provides a strong source of light and its reflection provides a secondary, softer illumination in the foreground. Against the darkness, he accentuates the major elements of the painting by using the moonlight as an outline with which he highlights the figures of the monks. A more diffuse light serves to emphasise the smooth-shafted columns of the temple and its architectural details such as the Corinthian capitals and the frieze of *bucrania* (a reference to the sacrifice of oxen).

This work would have appealed to connoisseurs of Claude. The inclusion of only part of the temple on the right recalls his *Coast View of Delos with Aeneas* (1672, National Gallery, London). However, here the Temple of Diana Nemorensis is shown in a ruined state, which is how it would have appeared to the many Grand Tourists who visited this site in the eighteenth century.[84]

---

83 Sir James George Frazer, *The Golden Bough, A Study in Magic and Religion*, London, 1922, p. 1 and passim
84 David H. Solkin, *Richard Wilson, The Landscape of Reaction*, Exhibition Catalogue, Tate Gallery, 1982, p. 192, cat. 77

5B *Figures by a Torrent in a Stormy Wooded Landscape*

This stormy subject, representing the quality of the sublime, appears to be an idealised rather than an identifiable view. The narrative content is detailed enough to suggest that it may have been based on a work of literature. The scene is framed on the left hand side by a rock face, while a cave and a group of trees is shown on the right. The eye is led by a river back towards the remains of a Roman aqueduct and behind it hills are just visible in the darkness. Above, the dark foliage of a tree masks the light of the moon to dramatic effect.

Forrester has captured a moment in time when a jagged flash of lightning strikes the tree in the right foreground, causing the main branch to crash into the river beneath. To the left a tragic scene unfolds; a woman is lying on the ground and appears to be dying. A man, wearing a red mantle, which streams out behind him, is starting to run for help. An older man remains with her, supporting himself with his staff. Two other small figures appear on the road, one in the middle distance driving a cow. Neither is aware of the drama. The disparate elements of this large painting are united by a compositional oval, linking the foreground figures to the fallen branch, the lightning, the upper part of the trees, the moonlit sky and the illuminated cliffs on the left. The broken branch and the dying woman in the foreground are both powerful reminders of the transience of life. These elements are paralleled by the ruined aqueduct, which recalls the past civilization of ancient Rome.

In terms of the recession, this painting owes a debt to Claude Lorrain. However, it is more reminiscent of the work of Gaspard Dughet, noted for his land storms. The damaged tree and mountainous landscape also show the influence of the Neapolitan painter, Salvator Rosa, whose work illustrates the quality of the sublime. Forrester may also have seen an engraving (William Woollett, 1761) of *The Destruction of the Children of Niobe* (Yale Center for British Art, New Haven), by Richard Wilson, which

Figure 22 Richard Wilson, *The Destruction of the Children of Niobe*, Yale Centre for British Art,
Paul Mellon Collection

had met with great critical acclaim when it was exhibited in London in 1760 (figure 22).[85] Alternatively like Wilson he may have looked directly back to the model of Poussin whose works such as the *Landscape with Pyramus and Thisbe,* (Städelsches Kunstinstitut, Frankfurt) were the ultimate inspiration for this model of the dramatic sublime (figure 23).

85 *Ibid.,* pp. 200 - 02, cat. 87

This scene is tightly painted, particularly noticeable in the silhouette of the foliage contrasting against the brightness of the moon. The use of colour is well balanced; the red of the man's mantle in the foreground is repeated in small touches in various other parts of the canvas, such as in the area of the cracked branch. The figure of the man running shows good use of foreshortening, attesting to the fact that Forrester had attended classes in life drawing in Rome. However, it is in the remarkable subtlety of the light effects that the artist shows his greatest skill; the variegated tones of light and dark make it a masterpiece of tenebrism.

(N.F.)

Figure 23 Nicholas Poussin, *Landscape with Pyramus and Thisbe,* Städelsches Kunstinstitut, Frankfurt
© Ursula Edelmann

6.

James Forrester

(circa 1730 – 1776)

Capuchin Monks by a Tomb at Lake Nemi

Oil on canvas

51 x 70 1/2 ins

130 x 179 cms

formerly signed on reverse of original canvas: "James Forrester pinxt Romae 1772"

Exhibited: *Into View: British Paintings from Private Collections,*

Gainsborough House, Sudbury, 1986, (no. 6)

This painting is very similar in subject to the moonlit scene with monks painted six years earlier, which was acquired by Lord Fitzwilliam (catalogue 5A). It is also a prospect of Lake Nemi, one of the crater lakes in the Alban Hills, and a favourite haunt of Gaspard Dughet in the seventeenth century. In antiquity Lake Nemi was dedicated to the goddess Diana. Virgil had referred to this smooth lake as the *Speculum Dianae,* the Mirror of Diana, which was mentioned in numerous guidebooks of the eighteenth century.

The foreground may show the gardens of the Capuchin monastery, close to the village of Genzano, which overlooks Lake Nemi. The three monks communicate a sense of spirituality as they go about their nocturnal prayers. They are shown wearing their distinctive habits,[86] one kneeling in front of a tomb, ornamented with a *bucranium.* Standing beside him, with his back to the lake, the figure of the monk appears to be an exact replica of the monk on the left of the Fitzwilliam painting.

---

86 Capuchins are a branch of the order of Franciscans, named from the *capuche* or cowl worn by them as their head-dress.

Figure 24 Richard Wilson, *Solitude*, The Glynn Vivian Art Gallery, Swansea

In the middle distance on the opposite side of the lake is a classical temple, similar to the Pantheon in Rome. This may have been an attempt by the artist to reconstruct the Temple of Diana Nemorensis in its complete state. Otherwise the scene is shown as entirely wooded; today the lake is still surrounded by woods of ilex and manna-ash. On the extreme left two cypress trees, associated with death, provide a strong vertical element in the painting. This is softened by the windswept tree, leaning outwards, a small romantic element in an otherwise calm, classical scene. The mood of the landscape comes close to that of Wilson's *Solitude* of 1762 (figure 24) which when it was engraved was accompanied by lines from James Thomson's *Seasons* which capture equally well the mystery, melancholy and awe of Forrester's landscape:

> These are the Haunts of Meditation, These
> The Scenes where antient Bards th' inspired Breath
> Estatic fel't and from this World retir'd.[87]

(N.F.)

---

87 Quoted in David H. Smolkin, *Richard Wilson, The Landscape of Reaction*, Exhibition Catalogue, Tate Gallery, London, 1982, p. 212

7.

Robert Carver
(circa 1730 – 1791)

Landscape with Ruins and Figures
Oil on canvas
38 ½ x 53 ins
98 x 134.5 cms

Robert Carver was one of the leading scene painters of the mid-eighteenth-century Dublin and London theatre and is one of the most interesting landscape artists of the generation of George Barret. Although born in Dublin his family, like Thomas Roberts' came from Waterford. His father Richard was also an artist by whom, however, only one picture, *A Landscape with Gentlemen Fishing and Shooting* (Ulster Museum) survives. He is known, however, to have painted overdoors at Howth Castle. Robert Carver studied initially with his father and subsequently at the Dublin Society Schools under Robert West. In 1754 he succeeded John Lewis (see catalogue 4) as scene painter at Smock Alley Theatre, moving later to work with Spranger Barry at the new theatre in Crow Street. Here he painted scenes for *The Orphan of China, The Indian Emperor* and *King Arthur*. However, his most successful set was for *A Trip to the Dargle* for which he painted "an Astonishing Effect of the Representation of the Waterfall of Powerscourt". This depiction of the most famous *leitmotif* of the picturesque in Ireland was echoed in a canvas painted a little later depicting a *Landscape with Figures by a Waterfall* (private collection). In 1762 with his pupil Edmund Garvey he visited Cork where he met James Barry. Between 1765 and 1768 Carver sent twenty pictures to the Society of Artists in Ireland from his home in Lazar's Hill. Despite initial success Carver felt unappreciated at home and in 1769 he departed for London after a musical benefit night at Crow Street Theatre raised funds for his trip.

Shortly after his arrival in London, Carver was appointed principal scene painter at

Figure 25 Robert Carver, *Landscape with Peasants and a Dog*,
Reproduction courtesy of the National Gallery of Ireland

Drury Lane by Garrick, probably acting on the advice of Spranger Barry. His innovative stage designs met with acclaim. His *Dublin Drop,* clearly an essay in the sublime style, was described by Edward Dayes as: "a representation of a storm on a coast with a fine piece of water dashing against some rocks and forming a sheet of foam truly terrific; ….compos[ing] a picture which would have done honour to the first artist, and will be remembered as the finest painting which ever decorated a theatre".[88] Carver worked at Drury Lane until 1774 when he followed Barry to Covent Garden after a dispute with Garrick. Here one of his great successes was his design for *The Castle of Andalusia* of 1781. In addition to his work in the theatre he painted at Vauxhall Gardens. Carver had sent work to the exhibitions of the Free Society in London from as early as 1765 when he still lived in Dublin. From 1770 he also exhibited at the Society of Artists of which he was elected President in 1778. Later he twice exhibited at the Royal Academy. When in 1770 his fellow Irish landscape painter George Mullins sent *A Cataract* to the Academy he gave Carver's address of Great Newport Street. The fact that Carver's pupil James B. Coy also studied in Dublin under Mullins suggests further contact between the two artists. Their approaches to landscape painting are, however, quite distinct with Mullins, in general, painting in a tighter more highly finished style. Carver is rather closer to Barret's work of about 1760 exemplified by works such as *Powerscourt Waterfall*, (National Gallery of Ireland) and at times he resembles John Butts although their

---

88 Edward Dayes, *The Works of the Late Edward Dayes*, London, 1805, (ed. R. Lightbown, 1971), p. 323

manner of painting figures is always quite distinct.

The two great models for landscape artists of the period were the Dutch seventeenth-century school and the Italianate vision of Claude. This was a reflection of the taste of patrons. In the collection of the Cobbe family at Newbridge House, for example, hung landscapes by both Hobbema and Gaspard Dughet.[89] Carver painted in both of these distinct styles although

Figure 26 Robert Carver, *A Classical Landscape*, Castle Ward, The Bangor Collection (The National Trust). Photograph: Photographic Survey, Courtauld Institute of Art

there are clear correspondences in his method in each idiom. A fine example of his Claudian mode *An Arcadian Landscape with Travellers* of 1764 (private collection) clearly evokes the Roman Campagna and may well be influenced by prints after Claude which circulated widely.[90] In other works such as *Landscape with Peasants and a Dog* (National Gallery of Ireland) (figure 25) the treatment of the landscape and in particular the handling of the trees looks back to the Dutch school. The present work is a pleasingly original, and seemingly quite deliberate, mixture of the Dutch and the Claudian. Two figures converse beside an altar or funerary monument which is marked indistinctly to give the impression of an inscription. Their gestures suggest earnest discussion. Indeed one of the hallmarks of Carver's art is this interaction, often accompanied by gesticulating, of two central figures. It can be seen in the National Gallery work (figure 25) and again in *A Classical Landscape* at Castleward (figure 26). To the right a magnificent classical building falls into decay. Certainly there is an

---

89 See Alistair Laing (ed.), *Clerics and Connoisseurs, An Irish Art Collection through Three Centuries*, London, (forthcoming, September, 2001)
90 See Crookshank / Glin / Laffan, pp. 26 - 29

Figure 28 Robert Carver, *Classical Landscape,* private collection.

element present of the *sic trasit* theme which Smolkin identifies in Richard Wilson.[91] This is paralleled elsewhere in Carver's work for example on the right hand side of the *Capriccio Landscape* (private collection) (figure 27) in which the fallen architrave is closely echoed. Perhaps the closest parallel, however, in the rest of Carver's oeuvre is with his *Classical Landscape* of 1766 (private collection) which is important as one of the only works which the artist signed in full. Again ruins dominate the right hand side of the composition with a view opening in the centre (figure 28).[92] The feeling of loss at the destruction of the civilisation which constructed these great buildings is a key element of the Arcadian myth and in the present work the figures by the tomb seem to tie it more specifically to the *Et in Arcadia Ego* motif, made famous by Poussin, signifying the presence of death even in the pastoral world.

So clearly the right hand side of the picture can be read as an evocation of the Arcadian myth of Claude. The left hand side, however, brings us, almost humorously, back to reality. In contrast to the open sky and the long view to the distant mountains it is densely wooded. A solitary fisherman (the very antithesis of the Golden Age where fishing was unknown) with his back to the viewer casts his line. His bright red coat effectively pulls our eye away from the scene on the right. Carver often composes his landscapes on a geometric basis. Here the canvas is divided neatly into two almost

91 David H. Smolkin, *Richard Wilson, The Landscape of Reaction*, Exhibition Catalogue, Tate Gallery, London, 1982, pp. 37 - 55
92 With Cynthia O'Connor, August 1983

Figure 27 Robert Carver, *Capriccio Landscape*, (detail) private collection.

detail of catalogue 7

exactly equal portions while there is a diagonal movement upwards from the seated fisherman via the standing figure in the central middle distance to the top of the buildings on the right. Similar fishermen with their backs to us are employed in the only known landscape by the elder Carver.

Carver's is a quite distinctive hand. He uses a full brush and there is often a lush warmth to the paint surface. His style is equally recognisable in either his Dutch or Italianate mode. Surprisingly few of Carver's paintings have survived with most of his dated landscapes coming from his period in Ireland. Clearly the demands placed on him by the London theatres and later, perhaps, by his administrative duties at the Society of Artists saw him produce fewer easel paintings. The clear correspondences

with his *Landscape with Peasants and a Dog* would perhaps suggest a date in the mid-1750s for the present work. The handling of the trees and similar recession towards the distant mountains are particularly close. However, many of the same features also appear in his Claudian *Arcadian Landscape* of 1764 where similarly oversized vegetation frames the foreground. Indeed in the 1760s Carver exhibited various works at the Society of Artists in Ireland with titles such as *Ruins and Figures* which could *Figures* which could conceivably correspond with the present work.

This landscape then presents us with a charmingly eclectic mix of the two styles of landscape painting available to an artist in Ireland in the middle of the eighteenth century. Seemingly in a quite knowing way Carver responds here to the debate on their relative merits articulated most strongly by Sir Joshua Reynolds.

> The Italian attends to the invariable, the great and general ideas which are fixed and inherent in universal Nature; the Dutch, on the contrary, to literal truth and a minute exactness of details, I may say, of Nature, modified by accident.[93]

Professor Edward McParland has defined much eighteenth-century Irish architecture by its quality of invigorating, libertarian, eclecticism seeing this as the great advantage of peripheral centres such as Dublin.[94] Many of his comments can be equally applied to Irish painting of the same period – van der Hagen is another case in point. In the present work Carver combines different modes of landscape art in a way which would have been inconceivable to London based artists such as Wilson and by so doing produces a work which is recognisably Irish.

(W.L.)

---

93 Joshua Reynolds, *The Idler*, no. 79, 20th Oct 1759
94 Edward McParland, "Eclecticism: the Provincial's Advantage" in *Irish Arts Review Yearbook*, 1991-1992, p. 213

8.

Hugh Douglas Hamilton

1739 - 1808

Bust-length Portrait of James Colyear Dawkins of Standlynch

Pencil and pastel in its original Italian carved and gilded neo-classical frame

9 x 7 ¾ ins

23 x 19.5 cms (oval)

Provenance: By descent through the family of the sitter to the Rev. E.H. Dawkins

Sold Christie's, London, 28th February, 1913, lot 10

(40 guineas to Edwards)

Literature: Walter Strickland, "Hugh Douglas Hamilton, Portrait-Painter*",*

in *The Second Annual Volume of the Walpole Society,* 1912 - 13, Oxford, 1913, p.105

Walter Strickland, *A Dictionary of Irish Artists*, Dublin, 1913, (1969), Vol. 1, p. 437

Anne Crookshank and the Knight of Glin, "Some Italian Pastels by Hugh Douglas

Hamilton", in *Irish Arts Review Yearbook,* 1997, Vol. 13, p. 69, no. 18

John Ingamells, *A Dictionary of British and Irish Travellers in Italy 1701 - 1800,*

Compiled from the Brinsley Ford Archive, New Haven and London, 1997, p. 284

Hugh Douglas Hamilton is the greatest of the many fine pastellists who learnt their art at the Dublin Society Schools and in his double portrait of Tresham and Canova (figure 29) produced one of the finest works on paper of the eighteenth century. He was born in 1739 the son of a wig maker of Crow Street, Dublin and studied at the Dublin Society Schools from 1750 to 1756 where he won several prizes and, according to a fellow student, was "remarkable for choosing, when drawing the human figure, the most foreshortened view, consequently the most difficult".[95] It seems likely that he also studied in the School of Ornament and a remarkable early work *Capriccio Title Page of Rocque's Survey of Kilkea, County Kildare,* shows his ability at handling architectural

---

95 John O'Keefe, *Recollection of the Life of John O'Keefe, Written by Himself,* London, 1862, Vol. 1, p. 12

Figure 29 Hugh Douglas Hamilton, *Antonio Canova in his Studio with Henry Tresham*,
Victoria and Albert Museum, London, V&A Picture Library

perspective. The drawing was commissioned in 1760 by the Earl of Kildare who was a patron of the Schools and whose mother Hamilton was also to draw.

In about 1764 Hamilton moved to London where after initial forays into history painting he soon established a successful practice with his small, oval portraits in pastel. "He could scarce execute all the orders that came in upon him and…in the evening of each day, a part of his occupation was picking and gathering up the guineas from amongst the bran and broken crayons…which in the hurry of the day he had thrown them."[96] Among his patrons were Sir Watkin Williams Wynn, (for whose house in London Thomas Roberts painted landscapes) and Lord Halifax whom he

96 Thomas James Mulvany, "Hugh Douglas Hamilton", in *Dublin Monthly Magazine*, Jan. – June 1842, p. 68 - 69

shows in a group portrait of 1767 flanked by his secretaries. Hamilton exhibited extensively at the Society of Artists and occasionally at the Free Society. In 1769 he sent two portraits to the Society of Artists in Dublin. Perhaps one of the finest of his portraits from this period is the group of the Rose family, which is dated 1775.

In 1778 Hamilton set off for Rome accompanied by his daughter with the seeming intention of developing his art in the direction of history painting. However, his *Diana and Endymion* (private collection) is the only subject picture he is known to have produced during his stay, with the rest of his oeuvre from his years in Italy consisting of portraits. Despite his failure to produce the hoped for subject paintings, as Anne Crookshank and the Knight of Glin note: "Rome, its antiquities and its contemporary neo-classical artists…all profoundly affected the development of [his] art".[97] Like Fagan who developed a rather sculptural technique in his portraits, no doubt derived from the classical statuary which he excavated, Hamilton reused motifs and poses from the antique in his figurative work.[98] Though he continued to work on a small scale he also produced, seemingly on the encouragement of his friend the sculptor John Flaxman, a remarkable series of large full-length pastels of visiting tourists. Among the most notable of these are the portraits of the Fifth Earl of Guilford (National Gallery of Art, Washington) and Jonas Langford Brooke (private collection) (see figure 4). Of a rather different character is his *Portrait of Frederick Hervey, Bishop of Derry on the Janiculum Hill* (National Trust, Ickworth).

The Earl Bishop continued his patronage of Hamilton who depicted him again in about 1790, this time in oil, showing him accompanied by his granddaughter in the gardens of the Villa Borghese (National Gallery of Ireland). His masterpiece, however, is the pastel of the Irish artist Henry Tresham in Canova's studio admiring the latter's *Cupid and Psyche* which Hamilton exhibited at the Royal Academy in 1791 (Victoria and Albert Museum, London). Hamilton stayed in Italy for some fourteen years, living

---

97 Anne Crookshank and the Knight of Glin, "Some Italian Pastels by Hugh Douglas Hamilton", in *Irish Arts Review Yearbook*, Vol. 13, 1997, p. 69
98 See the essay by Nicola Figgis above for further references.

mostly in Rome but also in Florence between 1783 and 1786, where he was elected a member of the *Academia del Disegno*. He also visited Venice and Naples where he painted a fine triple portrait of Lady Hamilton in the guise of the three muses. Together with Flaxman he toured the classical sites of Pompeii, Herculaneum and Paestum.

Returning to Dublin in 1792, Hamilton concentrated on oil painting. *Cupid and Psyche* (National Gallery of Ireland) (the subject no doubt inspired by Canova) was exhibited to great acclaim at the Society of Artists in 1800 and was described by the *Hibernian Magazine* as "perhaps the most perfect picture ever produced in this country".[99] Other important works from Hamilton's later period in Ireland include the *Portrait of Colonel Manserg St. George Mourning at his Wife's Tomb* (National Gallery of Ireland) which recalls in ways the elegant full-length pastel portraits executed in Italy. An important work, also exhibited in 1800, was *The Rev. Dean Kirwan Pleading the Cause of the Destitute Orphans* commissioned by the Governors of the Female Orphan House in Dublin and described at the time as a "masterpiece of excellence".[100] After so long in Italy Hamilton felt artistically isolated in Dublin and his letters to Canova frequently express his desire to return to Rome. He retired from painting in 1804 and devoted the last four years of his life to the study of chemistry, in particular the nature of pigments. Hamilton's daughter, Harriott, was an accomplished artist who finished some of her father's works after his death.

It is most likely that the present work was painted during Hamilton's stay in Florence. It is one of two portraits by the artist showing the young James Colyear Dawkins of Standlynch, Wiltshire on his Grand Tour. Dawkins, the nephew of James Dawkins, discoverer of Palmyra, was in Italy from 1783 to 1784 travelling with his Swiss governor, Bynion. The Reverend John Parkinson records meeting him in Florence on 13th December 1783, a date at which, as we have seen, Hamilton was also in the city.[101] Hamilton executed portraits of other members of Dawkins' circle in Florence, including

---

99   Strickland, Vol. 1, p. 431
100 *Dublin Evening Post*, June 1800, quoted *ibid.*
101 Crookshank / Glin, *op. cit.*, 1997, p. 69, n. 18

John Ramsay (son of the portrait painter) and the radical poet Robert Merry to whose *Arno Miscellany* both Alan Ramsay and Dawkins' tutor Bynion contributed.[102] Hamilton's other portrait of Dawkins is a rather more ambitious work, unfortunately now in ruinous condition (figure 30). An unusually large pastel it shows Dawkins reclining on a Roman sarcophagus in a setting suggesting the Villa Albani and was probably executed in Rome. The two portraits shared

Figure 30 Hugh Douglas Hamilton, *Reclining Portrait of James Colyear Dawkins of Standlynch*, (private collection) © Christie's Images Limited (2001)

the same provenance until they were dispersed at Christie's in 1913. Dawkins left Florence on 19th March 1784 (apparently in the company of Mrs Hannah Long, whose husband had died in Rome the previous August and whom he later married) leisurely making his way back to England. He was elected a Member of Parliament the same year serving until 1826. He died in 1843.

In this portrait Hamilton reverts to the oval format with which he had been so successful in London. However, compared to his earlier works it is a more finished, less sketchy work. The restrained choice of colours and simplicity of pose and setting reflect Hamilton's growing awareness of the international neo-classical movement. As Cullen notes his Italian pastels reveal a "new solidity and attention to the structure of the composition".[103] Preserved in its original frame the present portrait is a fine example of Hamilton's Italian period.

(W.L.)

---

102   Ingamells, p. 284; (see also the notes on Ramsay and Merry)
103   Fintan Cullen, "Hugh Douglas Hamilton in Rome, 1779 – 92", in *Apollo*, Vol. 115, 1982, p. 86

9.

Matthew William Peters, R.A.

(1741 - 1814)

Portrait of Lady Elizabeth Compton

Oil on canvas

30 x 25 ins

76 x 63 cms

Inscribed upper left: "Lady Elizabeth Compton daughter of

Charles 7th Earl of Northampton"

According to Manners formerly bore label inscribed: "Lady Elizabeth Compton,

married to Lord George Cavendish at age of 19,

given to her by her aunt Mary Isabella, Duchess of Rutland"

Engraved in mezzotint by J.R. Smith and published 24th February 1780

Provenance: Duchess of Rutland

Lady Elizabeth Compton (the sitter)

thence by descent to

Hon. Henry Cavendish

with W.H. Young, New York, 1928

W.A. Fisher Collection, Detroit

Howard Young Galleries, Inc., New York

Exhibited: Grosvenor Gallery 1889 and 1910

"One of the best known of Peters' portraits of "fair women", wrote Lady Manners, the artist's biographer, "is the radiant and beautiful half-length of Lady Elizabeth Compton, afterwards Lady Burlington."[104] Indeed it may be argued that the present work is Peters' portrait masterpiece and comparison between it and portraits of the same sitter by Reynolds and Romney show how at his best Peters could match the work of his finest contemporaries.

---

104   Lady Victoria Manners, *Mathew William Peters, R.A.*, London, 1913, p. 47

Figure 31 Mathew William Peters, *Self Portrait with Robert West*,
by courtesy of the National Portrait Gallery, London.

A personality of many contradictions, Peters was born on the Isle of Wight to Irish parents and grew up in Dublin where his father had set up in business as a seedsman in Capel Street, working for Lord Charlemont at Marino and publishing several treatises on agriculture. After a period in Dr Sheridan's school at which stage it seems he was destined for the Church, Peters embarked on his artistic career. He studied under Robert West whom he portrayed in a famous double portrait showing the master painting his pupil (National Portrait Gallery, London) (figure 31). This enormously refined work was executed when the artist was only sixteen and shows the high degree of sophistication in the handling of chalk by artists in West's circle.[105] After West's drawing academy was taken over by the Royal Dublin Society, Peters won a series of prizes and after a period working with Thomas Hudson in London he was sent by the Society to Italy with an allowance of thirty pounds a year. In Rome, Peters studied at the *Academia del Nudo* and at Batoni's private academy. He moved to Florence in 1763 where it is recorded that he studied Masaccio's frescoes in the Brancacci Chapel and like Hugh Douglas Hamilton twenty years later he was elected to the *Academia del Disegno*. Peters returned briefly to Dublin but settled in London where he became a member of the Society of Artists with whom he exhibited portraits until 1769 when he started to show at the Royal Academy. He retained his connections with Dublin, however, exhibiting at the Society of Artists in Ireland in 1768.

---

105   For an interesting discussion of this work see Noel Sheridan, in *NCAD 250, Drawings 1746 – 1996*, Dublin, 1996, pp. 8 - 9

Peters visited Italy again in 1771 escorting the Duke of Gloucester around the Pitti Palace and spending time in Venice. This was to prove particularly influential on his art as the colouring of his work is clearly derived from his careful study of the great Venetian masters of the sixteenth century gaining him the sobriquet "the English Titian".[106] From Venice he sent portraits in crayon to the Royal Academy. On his return from Italy, Peters started work on his controversial series of "pin ups" showing young women in states of *dishabillé*. His first work in this vein *A Lady in an Undress* was exhibited at the Royal Academy in 1776 and was followed the next year by *A Woman in Bed* which may be the work also entitled *Lydia* in the Tate Gallery.[107] The latter work was described by one contemporary critic as "fit for a bagnio", continuing "in its present position it seems to prevent the pictures around it being admired...for every man who has either his wife or daughter with him must for decency's sake hurry them away from that corner of the room".[108] These pictures were far more daring than anything previously shown in London, recalling the work of Greuze, which Peters had studied in Paris and were produced for a circle of aristocrats such as Lord Grosvenor who displayed *A Woman in Bed* behind a curtain. Peters had been a Freemason since 1769 which brought patronage from The Duke of Manchester and Lord Petrie, both grandmasters and it is in the context of this sophisticated, if risqué, coterie which these works must be understood. They clearly did little harm to Peters' professional standing and he was elected a member of the Academy in 1777.

Two years later, however, Peters embarked on a radical change in career. After a period of study at Exeter College, Oxford, in 1782 he was ordained an Anglican clergyman. He turned away from his earlier salacious work by which he was greatly embarrassed and in 1780 exhibited his *Angel Carrying the Spirit of a Child to Paradise,* producing other religious and sentimental works which earned him the description "Luke the saint, a man of gospel, art and paint".[109] He rose quickly within the church

---

106   For a full account of Peters' career in Italy see Nicola Figgis, "Matthew William Peters", in Ingamells, p. 762
107   See *Angels and Urchins, the Fancy Picture in Eighteenth-century British Art,* Exhibition Catalogue, Kenwood House, London, 1998, no. 74
108   Quoted in Crookshank / Glin, 1978, p. 98
109   Manners, *op. cit.,* p. 19

and was appointed chaplain both to the Prince Regent and to the Academy itself. Between 1786 and 1790, Peters worked on large canvasses for Boydell's Shakespeare Gallery illustrating scenes from the *Merry Wives of Windsor, Much Ado about Nothing* and *Henry VIII*. He also contributed five large canvases to the similar scheme for an Irish Shakespeare Gallery devised by James Woodmason but never brought to fruition.[110] His last exhibit at the Royal Academy was in 1785 and he resigned his membership three years later. Peters married in 1790 and accumulated a large fortune through preferment in the Church. Although best known for the erotic fancy pictures the majority of his oeuvre consists of portraits. He was particularly good with child portraits of which *Three Children Dressing Up* (National Trust) is a fine example. Strickland's assessment is worth quoting at length. "In his portraits he shows a strength and ease in painting, with good colour…Had he devoted his talents to portraiture instead of wasting them on his historical pictures and his ill-drawn, badly coloured angels and pious children by which he is best known, he would have been regarded, and taken his place, as one of the best painters of the English school."[111]

Indeed the present portrait confirms Strickland's assessment. It shows Lady Elizabeth Compton the only child of Charles Compton, 7th Earl of Northampton and his wife Lady Anne Somerset, daughter of the Duke of Beaufort. Lady Elizabeth was born in 1760. As the only child of the Earl of Northampton, Lady Elizabeth was a considerable heiress and on her marriage in 1782 to Lord George Cavendish much of the famous Compton collection of paintings passed to Chatsworth. Her husband George Cavendish was the youngest son of the 4th Duke of Devonshire and Lady Elizabeth was accordingly sister-in-law to Georgiana, the famous Duchess of Devonshire the friend of the Prince Regent, Sheridan and Fox. Although the relationship between Georgiana and Lady Elizabeth was not always cordial, the Duchess praised her activities for the Whig cause in the Westminster by-election of 1788.[112] After the coronation of William IV her husband was raised to the peerage as the Earl of Burlington, the title having

110   Robin Hamlyn, "An Irish Shakespearean Gallery", in *Burlington Magazine*, Vol. 120, 1978, pp. 515 - 29
111   Strickland, Vol. 2, p. 233
112   Amanda Foreman, *Georgiana, Duchess of Devonshire*, London, 1999, p. 205

previously been held by his maternal grandfather the great connoisseur and architect who had died without a male heir. A progressive politician in the Whig interest Lord George sat as an M.P. for ten parliaments before taking his seat in the House of Lords. Perhaps his most lasting memorial, however, is Burlington Arcade which he built in 1819 next to his London home Burlington House, now the Royal Academy.

Figure 32 J.R. Smith, *Portrait of Lady Elizabeth Compton* mezzotint after Mathew William Peters
© Copyright The British Museum

Like all of the Devonshire House set, Lady Elizabeth was painted by the leading portraitists of the day. From the mezzotint engraving after it by J.R. Smith (dated 24 February 1780) (figure 32) the portrait by Peters can be dated to the previous year. The ambiguous wording of the now lost inscription on the verso refers then to the sitter's age when the portrait was painted rather than at her marriage. It further states that it was commissioned by her aunt Mary Isabella Duchess of Rutland. Indeed at least three portraits of the Duchess by Peters are recorded as well as one of her husband Charles, who was Lord Lieutenant of Ireland from 1784 to his death in 1787. In addition the Duke bought two subject pictures from Peters *St John* and *A Country Girl* which

Figure 33 George Romney, *Portrait of a Lady*, identified as Lady Elizabeth Compton, (private collection)

Figure 34 Sir Joshua Reynolds, *Portrait of Lady Elizabeth Compton*, Photograph © Board of Trustees, National Gallery of Art, Washington, D.C.

were exhibited at the Royal Academy in 1777 and sent the artist to Paris to paint a copy of a work by Le Brun. Peters then was a natural choice when a portrait of Rutland's niece, Lady Compton was to be commissioned two years later. Slightly earlier Lady Elizabeth had been painted by Romney (a friend of Peters from their days in Italy), with sitting being recorded for 1776 and 1777. She sat again for him in 1782 and 1794. It is possible that the 1780s work is identical with that formerly on the London art market (figure 33). She was also painted by Hoppner. and, in full length, by Sir Joshua Reynolds (figure 34).

Peters is here at his most refined. The simple pose sets Lady Elizabeth against an open sky. Her elaborate hairstyle, adorned with pearls, is similar to that shown in the Reynolds portrait and reflects the latest fashion popularised by her soon to be sister-in-law, Georgiana.[113] The fully realised head with its strong sense of three-dimensionality is deliberately contrasted with the less substantial drapery and

Figure 35 Mathew William Peters, *Two Portrait Sketches*, private collection, © Christie's Images Limited (2001)

loosely sketched landscape background where the spirited brushwork is almost aggressively loose with marked use of impasto. The overall effect retains the spontaneous charm of the artist's portrait oil sketches (for example figure 35) where the artist's confidence of line is clearly apparent. The bright yellow of the bow and the red of her cheeks fully justify Anne Crookshank and the Knight of Glin's assessment of Peters as "the only eighteenth-century Irish painter who can be described as a colourist".[114] Indeed this quality of the portrait is rather emphasised by the mezzotint which, unusually for a work by that master engraver J.R. Smith, quite demonstrably fails to capture in black and white the charm of Peters' brush. In comparison to other portraits by Peters it has a sparkling vivacity and great immediacy of impact and as Manners well notes "[he] has well caught the bloom of youth and happiness while the colour is as fresh as if painted yesterday".[115]

(W.L.)

---

113 *Ibid.*, p. 37
114 Crookshank / Glin, 1978, p. 100
115 Manners, *op. cit.*, p. 46

10.
William Ashford, P.R.H.A.
(1746 – 1824)

A Pastoral Landscape in County Sligo with a Distant View of Cummin House

Oil on canvas

16 ¾ x 24 ins

42.5 x 61 cms

Signed and dated lower left: "W. Ashford 1784"

Although born in Birmingham, William Ashford spent almost his entire working life in Ireland and with George Barret and Thomas Roberts is one of the great artists of the Irish eighteenth-century landscape school. Born two years before Roberts, Ashford outlived him by some forty-six, living well into the nineteenth century and seeing the foundation of the R.H.A. of which he was the first president. Ashford arrived in Dublin in 1764 under the patronage of Ralph Ward the head of the Ordnance Department. He was appointed to the position of Clerk to the Comptroller of the Laboratory of the Ordnance for which he was paid £40 per annum. His job involved travelling around Ireland checking on the stocks of armaments and ammunition stored in the garrisons.

From 1767 Ashford exhibited at the Society of Artists in Dublin with his early exhibits consisting of flower pieces and still lifes, an attractive example of which A *Vase of Flowers,* is in the National Gallery of Ireland. It was not until 1772, however, that he showed his first landscape, winning the second premium from the Royal Dublin Society. The following year he won the first prize. In 1775 he exhibited at the Royal Academy and met with some critical success: "we don't remember this artist's name before in any exhibition; notwithstanding this, he is so far from being a novice in his profession, that, if he is young and attentive, he may well expect to reach the first form, in this department of painting".[116]

---

116   Unidentified newspaper cutting in the Courtauld Institute, London

For many years Ashford continued to exhibit in London, both at the Academy and at the Society of Artists of which he was elected a fellow in 1778. After the death of Thomas Roberts in the same year, Ashford completed his set of views of Carton and gradually began to dominate the Irish market for landscapes, being patronised by, among others, the Duke of Leinster, Viscount Fitzwilliam and the Earl of Drogheda. He was particularly successful at the rendering of trees, as one diarist commented of his Charleville series: "there is abundant scope for an exertion of the artist's genius in the delineation of foliage. The articulation is perfect and the colouring so beautifully rich, that I could with pleasure have spent hours in viewing them."[117] In addition to pure landscapes Ashford painted seascapes and the famous *Opening of the Ringsend Docks* of 1796 (National Gallery of Ireland) which shows effective handling of a crowd scene. In such works as *Jacques Contemplating the Wounded Stag* he also tried his hand at placing narrative scenes into landscape settings while the title of the lost work, *Lions and Leopards in a Landscape* suggests that he was imitating artists such as Stubbs and Ward.

In 1813 Ashford was elected President of the Irish Society of Artists and was instrumental in the foundation of the Royal Hibernian Academy of which he was voted the first president in 1823, this being a remarkable honour as landscape painting was then considered the lowest rung of the profession. From about 1792 Ashford lived in a house in Sandymount which his friend the great architect James Gandon had built for him. A miniature portrait by John Comerford gives a good impression of the artist in later years (figure 36). He died in 1824.

The present landscape is an attractive example of Ashford's middle period and is the only work known to date from the year 1784. It depicts an open landscape with, in the foreground, a simple mud dwelling next to a ford in a stream. Outside is a charming group of figures and animals with fowl being led by a woman. Our eye is

---

117   Crookshank / Glin, 1978, p. 136

led into the picture by the path and, one of the artist's favourite motifs, figures seen from behind travelling into the distance. To the right of the middle ground stands a more solidly built cottage with smoke pouring from a chimney. In the far background we can see a fine Georgian mansion nestling at the foot of a distinctive low mountain range. The painting has a wider horizon than many of Ashford's works which, together with the large expanse of sky gives it a bright open feeling. An old plaque on the frame describes the subject as "A Pastoral Scene; said to be in County Sligo with a distant View of Cummin House, the residence of John Ormsby Esq". This identification seems plausible. The Ormsbys were settled at Cummin House from at least 1672, the date of the will of Anthony Ormsby, preserved in the Public Records Office in Belfast. Sligo (and the north-west of Ireland generally) was rarely visited by artists of the period (although Thomas Roberts is known to have painted in Donegal) and if the picture does indeed show Cummin House it is one of the very few surviving eighteenth-century views of County Sligo.[118] Ashford travelled the length of the country for his work with the Ordnance and is known to have painted in County Cavan, not far away. It is quite likely that on one such journey he was commissioned by the Ormsbys to paint a view of their demesne.

Figure 36 John Comerford, *Portrait of William Ashford, P.R.H.A.*, reproduction courtesy of the National Gallery of Ireland

Stylistically the work fits in well with other Ashfords of the same period. Perhaps the

---

118 See the maps giving the distribution of identified views in paintings and drawings listed in the catalogues of the National Gallery of Ireland and in Elmes' *Catalogue of Topographical Prints*, in P.J. Duffy, "The Changing Rural Landscape, 1750 – 1850; Pictorial Evidence", in Raymond Gillespie and Brian Kennedy (eds), *Ireland, Art into History*, Dublin, 1994, p. 30.

Figure 37 William Ashford, *Landscape with Haymakers,*
private collection

closest comparison is with his *Landscape with Haymakers and a Distant View of a Georgian House* (figure 37). This has been dated to the same period (1780 – 1785) and again shows an open landscape with rustic figures in the foreground and a mansion in the distance.[119] The handling of the mountains in the two works is particularly close. Interestingly two views of Mount Kennedy House which are dated 1785, the year after the *Cummin House,* are of identical measurements although this was not to be a size that Ashford used again in his career. An unknown critic writing in 1800 described a work by the artist in terms which could equally be applied to the present landscape. "The colours are natural, the verdure is warm and mellow…the shadows on the water are broad and deep…the skies cool and pleasant….The union of the picture is so perfect and it is every where finished with so much solidity, judgement and beauty that we leave it each time with regret and return to it with fresh pleasure."[120]

(W.L.)

119   Anne Crookshank "A Life Devoted to Landscape Painting, William Ashford (circa 1746 – 1824)", in *Irish Arts Review Yearbook*, Volume 11, 1995, pp. 119 – 30, catalogue number 81
120   Quoted *ibid.*, p. 124

11.

Thomas Roberts

(1748 – 1778)

A Frost Piece

Oil on canvas

39 x 54 ins

99 x 137 cms

Exhibited: Probably Society of Artists, Dublin, 1769, no. 70, *A Frost Piece,*

or no. 65, *A Winter Piece*

The most brilliant Irish landscape painter of the eighteenth century, Thomas Roberts was born in Waterford in 1748. His father was a leading architect designing both Protestant and Catholic cathedrals in the city and several mansions including the forecourt of Curaghmore. After receiving a basic education in his native town he entered the Dublin Society Schools studying under James Mannin. In 1763, his first year at the Schools, he won a premium together with further awards in 1768, 1772 and 1777.

In addition to his time at the Schools, Roberts studied with the landscape artists John Butts and George Mullins, the latter of whom had Waterford connections. According to Pasquin, while living with Mullins at the Horse and Magpie Inn in Temple Bar, Roberts made his pocket money by "painting the black eyes of those persons who had been fighting and bruising each other in his master's tap-room on the previous evening".[121] Certainly he gave Mullins' address when exhibiting at the Society of Artists in Ireland between 1766 and 1768, thereafter living at 2 Dame Street. The style of master and pupil can easily be confused and it is likely that they collaborated. It has been suggested, for example, that the young Roberts may have had a hand in the four

---

121   Pasquin, p. 7

important pictures commissioned from Mullins by the Earl of Charlemont (National Gallery of Ireland).[122] A pair of pictures in the E.S.B. House in Dublin seems to have been painted one by Mullins the other by Roberts. The Roberts, showing the Sugar Loaf includes a white horse which became something of a feature in his work. While there are many similarities between the two landscapes, from an early age the young Roberts clearly outshone his master. Pasquin goes on to note that Roberts "gained more reputation as a landscape painter than any other Irishman".[123]

In his short life Roberts exhibited fifty-six paintings at the Society of Artists and his work was commissioned by the leading Irish aristocrats of the period including the Duke of Leinster, Viscount Powerscourt the Earl of Bessborough and the Earl of Ross. He also provided two landscapes for the staircase of Sir Watkin Williams Wynn's town house in London, which survive *in situ*. Early exhibited works included pictures of storms at land and sea in which the influence of Vernet is apparent. However, the bulk of his surviving work can be divided into three categories: topographical works such as *A View of Ballyshannon* (private collection), idealised landscapes and (a genre of which he made something of a speciality) sets of view paintings showing the seats and demesnes of the nobility. Notable examples of the latter include his set of four canvasses of Lucan House (National Gallery of Ireland). These show Roberts' love of half-lights, figures taking an evening walk by the river with the long shadows indicating the approaching darkness. They also use water with great skill, both the turbulent effect of a weir and the quiet beauty of the still flowing stream. Of equal importance is his magnificent set of views of Carton. One of these is dated 1776 and in that year Roberts is recorded in Bath seeking a cure for his consumption. The drawing master and pastellist, John Warren writing from Bath to Lord Bessborough's agent, Andrew Caldwell on 22nd July noted: "on hearing through my father that Roberts was come to Bristol I went there to find him so emaciated that he shocked me severely but have great pleasure in acquainting you that he has already rec'd great

122   Michael Wynne, "Thomas Roberts, 1748 – 1778", in *Irish Arts Review Yearbook*, Vol. 10, 1994, p. 143
123   Pasquin, *op. cit.*

benefit". He goes on to discuss his illness in detail and concludes that among all painters of landscapes that he has seen in the British Isles he thought "Roberts exceeds any".[124] Three of the Carton works were exhibited at the Society of Artists between 1775 and 1777 but by this time the artist was already dying. He travelled to Portugal and died in Lisbon in 1778 at the age of just thirty. The Carton commission was transferred to William Ashford.

Roberts' landscapes are crisply painted with a particular sensitivity for capturing the fall of light. Unlike some landscape artists he is extremely competent at painting figures which enliven many of his compositions, be they labourers, shepherds, pilgrims or the Duke and Duchess of Leinster stepping into their boat. One of his trademarks is the emphasis placed on horses, often acting as the focal point to the composition. Interestingly the only non-landscape painting by Roberts is the horse portrait, *Sir William (A Barb) in the Possession of Gerald Fitzgerald* (private collection). In one of the landscapes painted for Wynn's house in St James' Square Roberts introduces into the background the abbey of Castle Dermot and an Irish round tower and his work bears witness to the growing interest in early Irish remains. Indeed Roberts contributed drawings to Grose's *Antiquities of Ireland* and copies of further drawings survive in the Beranger album. Pasquin writes: "there was an elegance and a gentleness in the manners of Mr Roberts" and both qualities are noticeable in his art. Reviewing Roberts' oeuvre one cannot but be impressed by the variety of his work from stormy drama to quiet pellucid lake and river scenes with ruins in the background. His figures and animals, his delicate trees, his shafts of sunlight and his storm clouds are all brilliantly portrayed.

We have long noted the similarities between landscapes by Roberts and those of the seventeenth-century Dutch school. Many such were hung in the great houses of Ireland and would have been available for an artist to study. Quite what pictures

---

124   Philip MacEvansoneya, "An Irish Artist Goes to Bath, Letters from John Warren to Andrew Caldwell, 1776 – 1784", *Irish Architectural and Decorative Studies, the Journal of the Irish Georgian Society*, Vol. 11, 1999, p. 36

Roberts may have looked at or exact lines of influence have, however, been more difficult to establish. A work recently on the Amsterdam art market by Joris van der Hagen strikes us as so close to Roberts' work that there may be a possible connection.[125] Formerly attributed to Jacob Koninck it shows the latter's wide horizon line and large expanse of sky while the colouring is extremely close to

Figure 38 Willem van der Hagen, *A Winter Landscape*, private collection

Roberts. Works such as his *Castle Waterhouse, County Fermanagh* (private collection) seem to derive directly from models such as this. While the links between Joris and Willem van der Hagen remain obscure and (despite Strickland's confusion there is no evidence that the former visited Ireland) it is tempting to suppose that Roberts may have seen similar pictures.

Without doubt one of the greatest masterpieces of eighteenth-century Irish landscape art, *A Frost Piece* shows a quite different side of Roberts' art to the more familiar landscapes infused with soft, golden light. A group of cottages with icicles hanging from the thatch form the background for a gentleman out shooting with his dogs and servant and a cart driven by a man with a flock of sheep. Rather incongruously to their left a bearded, hatted elderly hermit-like figure guided by a dog on a lead enters his makeshift dwelling. Elsewhere, as in *the View of Slane Castle* (private collection) Roberts introduces similar figures derived from Italian artists such as Rosa and

125   Sotheby's 8th May 2001, lot 59. We are grateful to Baukje J.L. Coenen for discussing this picture with us.

Figure 39 Thomas Roberts, *A Land Storm*, private collection

Magnasco and indeed they are also to be found in Barret. The sportsman is frozen stiff clasping his arms in the cold and even the dog's breath is carefully painted. Again the influence of Dutch art is apparent with the subject recalling the iconography of Winter in sets of the four seasons. An immediate parallel may be found, however rather closer to home in a small panel by Willem van der Hagen (see figure 38). One of a pair of paintings this is the only other specifically winter landscape of the period known to us and contains many of the same elements as the Roberts.

The painting is a particularly remarkable achievement as it seems to be one of the earliest known paintings by the artist executed when he was only twenty-one years old. It seems almost certain that it was one of two works exhibited in the Society of Artists in 1769, either number 65 *A Landscape with Figures, A Winter Piece* or number 70 *A Frost Piece*. While it is possible that it was painted later in the artist's career it is difficult to believe that he would not have exhibited such an important landscape and there is no record of the later exhibition of a picture with a suitable title. It is possible to partially reconstruct Roberts' thirteen exhibits in the Society of Artists for 1769. They certainly included *A View of Rathfarnham* Castle, a slightly unusual work in his oeuvre for its genre element. Two works entitled *A Land Storm with a Waterfall* and *A Land Storm* (see figure 39) may also be identified with some certainty. In addition he exhibited a view of the Tinnahinch mountains and a moonlight scene. It seems that this was the year in which Roberts was confidently establishing himself as an artist deliberately displaying to potential clients his versatility in different genres of landscape. Interestingly in 1769 he sent more paintings for exhibition than in any other year of his short career. Clearly the tactic worked and as we have seen commissions flowed in. There was little competition in Dublin in that year. Barret was working in London and Ashford had not yet exhibited a landscape. The only landscape of comparable quality in the Dublin Society of Artists of that year was Fisher's stunning *View of Killarney, from Lord Kenmare's Park* (private collection), one of the finest topographical pictures of the eighteenth century but slightly old fashioned when compared to the Roberts.[126] The quietly beautiful composition and execution of the present work is almost unparalleled in Irish painting. However, Roberts should not be viewed in an Irish context alone but should now, like his predecessor Willem van der Hagen, take his place prominently in the annals of European landscape art.

(A.O.C. & K. of G.)

---

126 See Crookshank / Glin / Laffan, pp. 36 - 42

12.

Robert Fagan

(1761 – 1816)

Portrait of Marianne, Lady Acton with her Children, Richard, Charles and Elizabeth

Oil on canvas

63 ins x 65 ins

160 x 165 cms

Signed, dated and inscribed: "painted by Robert Fagan,

His Britannic Majesty's Consul General for Sicily 1809"

Provenance: by descent through the sitter's family to Lord Acton,

Aldenham, Shropshire; thence by descent to his grand-daughter the

Hon. Mrs Douglas Woodruff

Exhibited: Royal Academy, London, 1815, (no. 434)

Literature: W.G. Strickland, *A Dictionary of Irish Artists*, Dublin, 1913,

(1969), Vol. 1, p. 330

Anne Crookshank and the Knight of Glin, *Irish Portraits, 1660 – 1860,*

London, 1969, pp. 19 - 20, and p. 65; illustrated fig. 11

Raleigh Trevelyan, "Robert Fagan, an Irish Bohemian in Italy", in *Apollo,*

Vol. LXCVI, Oct. 1972, p. 308; illustrated fig. 24

Mark Bence-Jones, *The Catholic Families,* London, 1992; illustrated p. 101

William Laffan, *Robert Fagan in Sicily, The Acton Family Portrait,*

Pyms Gallery, London, 2000

Roland Hill, *Lord Acton*, New Haven and London, 2000, illustrated

Robert Fagan is with James Barry and Hugh Douglas Hamilton the finest of the Irish figurative painters who worked in Italy in the eighteenth century. Indeed his remarkable life story and the etiolated sculptural technique he pioneered make him

one of the most appealing of all Irish artists. Although born in London in 1761 where his Cork-born father had a successful business as a baker Fagan always defined himself as Irish. At the age of twenty he entered the Royal Academy Schools where he studied under Bartolozzi. After his father's death in 1783 he set off for Rome with intermediate stops in Paris and Flanders. He was to spend the rest of his life in Italy combining careers as art dealer, archaeologist and diplomat as well as a painter. Not surprisingly his oeuvre is small - only some twenty portraits are known. In Rome he knew the Irish sculptor Christopher Hewetson, was patronised by the Bishop Earl Hervey and Prince Augustus and produced elegant but always striking portraits of grand tourists (see for example figure 5). After the second French occupation of Rome Fagan was forced to leave. His political activities had incurred the displeasure of the Vatican and in 1807 by direct instruction of Napoleon he was given three days to leave the city for Palermo. Accompanying the Fagan family to Sicily was the young William Baker, heir to Bayfordbury in Hertfordshire who had fallen in love with Fagan's fifteen-year old daughter Estina and whose family in 1809 helped secure him the post of Consul General for Sicily.

The present portrait dates from the same year and is the key work of Fagan's late period. Set on a terrace flanked by curtains and a red drape Marianne, the young wife of Sir John Acton, gently cradles her daughter Elizabeth with her sons Richard and Charles on either side. In the distance is a view of the coastline near Palermo with Etna just visible on the horizon. The pyramidal form of the composition links the group together in an image of familial tenderness. Although Waterhouse makes the bold claim that Fagan was "the only British portrait painter who deliberately adopted a neo-classic style"[127] he was wholly ignored in a comprehensive survey of the subject as recently as 1966.[128] This oversight can partly be explained by the great rarity of his paintings, which in very many cases have remained, until recently, in the families of their original owners. His *Self Portrait with his Second Wife* (Hunt Museum, Limerick)

---

127   Ellis Waterhouse, *The Dictionary of British 18th-Century Painters in Oil and Crayons*, Woodbridge, 1981, p.122
128   David Irwin, *English Neoclassical Art, Studies in Inspiration and Taste*, London, 1966

has since become an almost iconic representation of the romantic artist. Clearly related to Barry's self portraits its air of defiant pride, swagger and gaze of almost cold contempt defines Fagan as an artist whose capacity to flaunt convention was allied to a world wise and highly suggestive modernity. His *Portrait of a Lady as Hibernia* (private collection) includes a harp with broken strings, a wolf hound and the inscription in Gaelic *Erin go Bragh*. This demands to be read as Fagan's identification of himself as an Irish artist mourning a romantic Ireland lost through the Act of Union. Indeed as with Barry, whose Cork heritage he shared, he often incurred the displeasure of his aristocratic patrons by his fiery Irish temperament and espousal of republican ideals.

Sir John Acton whose family is portrayed here was born in Besançon in 1736 where his father had settled after marrying a French bride and converting to Catholicism. After a period in the French navy he entered the service of the Grand Duke of Tuscany. In 1778 he was appointed to reorganise the Neapolitan fleet and rose to become prime minister of Naples. His rise to power was facilitated by his friendship with Queen Maria Carolina, together they were to effectively rule the kingdom for the next quarter of a century. In concert with the British ambassador Sir William Hamilton, Acton attempted to formulate an Italian league backed by the British against the French. In 1800 Acton (long a bachelor) had surprised the court by marrying his thirteen-year-old niece Marianne, having obtained a papal dispensation.[129] Sir William and Lady Hamilton were witnesses to the ceremony in the royal chapel in Palermo. To mark the marriage and his own capture of the French frigate the *Guillaume Tell,* Nelson hosted a ball on board his flagship the *Foudroyant* "two spacious rooms were made on deck, with divisions of billowing silk. The masts were also clad in silk and the guns removed. Little chocolate tables took their place."[130] It seems that Acton was prompted to his late decision to marry by his inheritance from his cousin Richard of the family baronetcy and the Aldenham estate in Shropshire and the consequent need to produce an heir.

---

129   Family tradition recounts that the thirteen-year old Marianne hid under a piano when told that she was to marry her sixty-three year old uncle and had to be coaxed out with a box of chocolates.
130   Flora Fraser, *Beloved Emma, The Life of Lady Hamilton*, London, 1986, p. 257

Figure 40 François-Xavier Fabre, *Maréchale Clarke with her Children*, Musée Marmottan, Paris

The Acton family portrait is proudly inscribed: "Painted by Robert Fagan, His Britannic Majesty's Consul General for Sicily 1809". He was appointed to this position on 7th June so the picture can most likely be dated to the second half of the year. Naturally given their respective positions Fagan and Acton would have had frequent diplomatic contact and the painting may well have been painted as an act of friendship or as a way of securing Acton's support in his dealings with Queen Carolina. Interestingly the only other portrait that Fagan is known to have painted in Sicily is *The Children of Lord Amherst* (National Gallery of Ireland). Amherst had succeeded to the position of Ambassador to the court and on 2nd August 1809 (when Fagan was presumably at work on the Acton portrait) he had hosted the marriage of Estina, Fagan's daughter to William Baker.[133]

The sources for Fagan's distinctive style have been sought in contemporary artists such as Fabre, Appiani and Tischbein.[134] Little attention, however, has previously been paid to his artistic development. The clear shift in his style after his famous self portrait of 1803 has been misunderstood. His later style is characterised by Trevelyan as "stile più rigido"[135] which is, I would argue, the exact opposite of the case. Compared to

---

133   In is interesting to note in this connection that Fagan had previously painted Lady Hamilton, wife of Amherst's predecessor (private collection).

134   Anne Crookshank and The Knight of Glin, *Irish Portraits, 1660 – 1860*, London, 1969, p. 65

135   Raleigh Trevelyan, Robert Fagan; un inglese in Sicilia", in *Kalos*, V, 6, November / December 1993, p. 16

rigorously sculptural early works such as the Miss Emily Manley (private collection)[136] both the Acton and Amherst portraits are much more freely painted. Fagan is here at his most original and indeed modern. He combines several elements of his own self-portrait in the painting. A curious stillness and theatricality of composition are common to both pictures while the direct gaze of Lady Acton echoes Fagan's own. The originality of the portrait can be best seen by comparing it to two other works of the same years Fabre's *Maréchale Clarke with her Four Children* (Musée Marmottan, Paris) (figure 40) dated to the following year, 1810 and Gérard's portrait of Julie Bonaparte with her children (National Gallery of Ireland) (figure 41) dated to 1808 - 09. Both works are masterpieces of the new French style pioneered by David but seem overly static and formal in comparison to the Acton portrait which by contrast has a direct

Figure 41 François Gérard, *Portrait of Julie Bonaparte with her Children*, reproduction courtesy of the National Gallery of Ireland

and remarkably modern appeal as an image of maternal love comparable to Vigée Le-Brun's *Self Portrait with her Daughter* (Louvre). Clearly the favourite painter of Marie-Antoinette would have been a model to follow at the court of her sister. Indeed the pose of Marianne holding her youngest child rather echoes Fagan's portrait of his second wife (private collection) (figure 42). Both images project an unsuspected tenderness and warmth slightly in conflict to what we know of the artist's character.

136   See Crookshank / Glin / Laffan, pp. 48 - 51

Figure 42 Robert Fagan, *Portrait of his Second Wife and Child*, private collection

That Fagan in Sicily was in the vanguard of the most advanced artistic movement of his day can be shown by a comparison with Josph Abel's *Portrait of Countess Maria Theresia von Fries* with her children in the Germanisches Nationalmuseum, Nuremberg (figure 43). Painted two years after the Acton Family Portrait it shows quite remarkable similarities with it. One of the defining elements of neo-classicism was its international element. Far from being artistically isolated in Sicily, Fagan was anticipating trends in European painting in its move from eighteenth-century neo-classicism to a softer empire style.[135]

The frankness of approach we have noted in the Acton Portrait belies an element of symbolic narrative within the image. Lady Acton seems to take on the iconography of *Caritas* which Reynolds had exploited in his portrait of Lady Cockburn (National Gallery, London) exhibited at the Royal Academy just seven years before Fagan entered the Academy schools. This iconography is combined with an identification of

---

135   Abel was in Rome from 1801 to 1807 where he could very well have known Fagan.

Lady Acton with Venus suggested by the bird proffered by her younger son in the reverential posture of an *offrans* on genuflected knee. The fact that Lady Acton is shown dressed *all'antica* while her children are shown in contemporary clothes encourages this emblematic reading. One detail which has not been commented on before, is the carving on the almost throne-like *tessara* on which Lady Acton sits. It is directly derived from a famous classical relief depicting Orpheus and Eurydice of which three versions are known, in the Louvre, Naples and in the Villa Albani in Rome.[136] Fagan had used this motif before in a series of grisailles commissioned by Lord Berwick for Attingham Park where it appears on the south wall of the outer library, although

Figure 43 Josph Abel, *Portrait of Countess Maria Theresia von Fries with her Children*, Nuremberg, Germanisches National Museum

without the figure of Mercury at the left (figure 44). One can only wonder if this sad scene of leave-taking had any personal significance to artist or sitter; perhaps more likely it is generically symbolic of marital love.

Two years after the portrait was painted Sir John Acton died. Marianne who had previously never left Italy departed for England and settled on the family estate of Aldenham, Shropshire, coincidentally only a few miles from Attingham, home to Fagan's grisailles. Her eldest son, Richard inherited the baronetcy. Despite the children's Cambridge education they were both drawn back to Italy. Richard, like his

---

136   See P. Bol, *Forschungen zur Villa Albani, Katalog der antiken Bildwerke*, Berlin, 1989, Vol. 1, no. 146

Figure 44 Robert Fagan, *Grisaille of Orpheus and Eurydice*,
(The National Trust, Attingham Park)
The Berwick Collection; (The National Trust)
Photograph: Photographic Survey,
Courtauld Institute of Art

father, entered the service of the Kingdom of the Two Sicilies and built the Villa Acton overlooking the Bay of Naples. He married the daughter of the Duke of Dalberg but died tragically young in 1837 when "according to family legend [his wife] to punish him for gambling, told the servants at the Hôtel Dalberg not to let him in when he returned one wintry night from the gambling tables; with the result that he died of pneumonia".[137]

Charles the younger son was clearly rather different in character to his brother. After Cambridge he went to Rome to study for the priesthood. He rose rapidly in the church and at the age of forty-one was appointed the youngest cardinal in the Sacred College. Although King Ferdinand II of the Two Sicilies was keen for him to be appointed Archbishop of Naples he declined and lived with his mother in Rome. In 1845 he was given the honour of being the only witness to the meeting of Pope Gregory XVI and Tsar Nicholas. At one point Marianne sold her jewels "to keep up the state required of him as a Prince of the Church and to provide money to his numerous charities".[138] In 1869, sixty years after Fagan's portrait Marianne welcomed Richard's son, John, recently created Lord Acton, to Rome for the Vatican Council.

137 Mark Bence-Jones, *The Catholic Families*, London, 1992, p. 167
138 *Ibid.*

As is well known Fagan's life ended miserably. Ill, and overwhelmed by the financial problems that had dogged him throughout his life he committed suicide by throwing himself out of a window in Rome on the 26th August 1816. The previous year he had made a final visit to London. This may well have been to clear his name with the authorities who were troubled by his behaviour. "You have so far departed from the strict line of the consular functions, as to lend yourself to be a party to political discussions with the governments in several parts of Italy" wrote Lord Bathurst.[139] Coincidentally in the same year the Acton portrait which Marianne had brought with her from Italy was exhibited at the Royal Academy. In 1823, after the death of William Baker, Fagan's daughter Estina married Lady Acton's brother Francis thus bringing together the families of painter and sitter of the portrait.

There is a rather touching postscript to the story of the Acton family portrait. Marianne, widowed at an early age had, shortly after her return to England, embarked on a liaison with a French royalist exile by whom she bore a son. For this indiscretion at her death many decades later in 1873 her grandson the first Lord Acton refused to erect a funerary tablet in her memory. His daughter later remembered Marianne's ghost haunting Aldenham at night "but it was said that when a memorial plaque was finally put up…she was not seen again".[140]

(W.L.)

---

139   Raleigh Trevelyan, "Robert Fagan, an Irish Bohemian in Italy", in *Apollo*, Vol. LXCVI, October, 1972, p. 308
140   Roland Hill, *Lord Acton*, New Haven and London, 2000, p. 249. I am grateful to Anne Thornton-Norris for bringing this recent publication to my attention.

William Sadler
(circa 1782 – 1839) (catalogue 13 – 14)

William Sadler has long been unfairly dismissed as one of the "poor relations" of Irish art history. However, as the recent discovery of his *Battle of Waterloo* (private collection) has shown he was a far more accomplished artist than he has been usually portrayed. There are admittedly difficulties in defining his oeuvre satisfactorily. He very rarely signed his pictures and his sons continued to work in his style after his death producing from a veritable production line many of the lesser works which are unfairly credited to him and detract from the achievement of his finest work.[141]

The few known facts of Sadler's life can be summarised briefly. His father, also William, was an artist who, though English-born, studied at the Dublin Society Schools and was patronised by the La Touche banking family. Hardly anything survives of the elder Sadler's work. His son was born in or about 1782 and lived and worked in Dublin throughout his life. He contributed to various exhibitions, including the Royal Hibernian Academy, between 1809 and 1833. In 1838 the auctioneer C. Bennett sold the "entire of last year's paintings", including copies of old masters, an *Eruption of Mount Vesuvius, Burning of the Royal Exchange, Wreck of the Killarney, Burning of the Arcade in College Green* and a number of small views of Dublin. He died at his home in Manders Building, Ranelagh in 1839.

An important group of battle paintings including the *Waterloo* has recently been identified which show greater ambition than the small views. The *Waterloo* in particular is a very strong work full of dash and vigour. As Strickland noted, and as the list of paintings sold at Bennett's indicates, Sadler had a predilection for scenes of conflagration and a strong taste for the dramatic. He also painted scenes of journalistic

---

141   See most recently, Crookshank / Glin / Laffan, pp. 52 – 60

interest such as the *Revenue Raid* and the *Search for Michael O'Dwyer* and some fine topographical landscapes of which the *Provost's House* (National Gallery of Ireland) is a good example. However, Sadler is perhaps at his most charming in his views of Dublin, often painted from a vantage point close to Island Bridge. Works such as *The Pigeon House* (National Gallery of Ireland) (figure 45) are

Figure 45 William Sadler, *The Pigeon House, Dublin,* reproduction courtesy of the National Gallery of Ireland

charming evocations of early nineteenth-century Dublin. In it particular attention is paid, as is often the case, to the varied staffage, soldiers, dock workers and passengers. A chronology for his work is almost impossible to establish but it is likely that paintings such as the set of landscapes of Killua Castle are early works and the more romantic (and ambitious) pictures such as the series of battle scenes date from later in his career.[142] The only correctly signed work by Sadler known to this author is a fine *View of a Church Interior* (private collection) in the manner of seventeenth-century artists such as Saenredam. This is signed and dated 1812, in Saenredam's usual manner on a tombstone in the church's pavement.[143] While most of Sadler's works are painted on small mahogany panels his larger paintings are sometimes on canvas. Sadler acts as an important link between the eighteenth-century tradition of landscape and the romanticism of his pupil James Arthur O'Connor.[144]

---

142   See Wanda Ryan-Smolin, "William Sadler's Views of Killua Castle, Co. Westmeath" in *Irish Arts Review Yearbook*, Vol. XII, 1996, pp. 66 - 70

143   The specificity of this signature tends to confirm the assumption that it is a unique occurrence in Sadler's oeuvre. It may be noted, however, that Sadlers occasionally appear on the art market with signatures added.

144   For the relationship between Sadler and O'Connor see Strickland, Vol. 1, p. 317. Strickland repeats this but less categorically in his life of O'Connor, Vol. 2, p. 179.

13.
William Sadler
(circa 1782 – 1839)
Travellers in a Lake Landscape
Oil on panel
8 ½ x 13 ins
21.5 x 33 cms

Sadler was primarily a Dublin artist. Although he painted frequent views of Killarney one wonders how often he actually visited Kerry. The bulk of his landscape oeuvre can be divided between views of Dublin (see catalogue 14) and those of the nearby Wicklow mountains. Sometimes as in a panel showing the military road by the Sugarloaf Sadler is topographically precise, on other occasions as with some of his Dargle views the setting is more generic. Here the location seems to be Lough Dan with in the foreground a man pointing out a gate to his female companion. Cattle rest on a rise in the ground to the right and in the middle distance at the edge of the lake can be seen a sizeable mansion. The excellent condition of the panel allows us clearly to see Sadler's typical blend of smooth finishing in the sky and background and lumped impasto for the vegetation. The warm palette with soft reflections of the mountains in the lake give a gentle yet glowing appeal to the work. The panel is preserved in its original Morland frame.

(W.L.)

14.

William Sadler

(circa 1782 – 1839)

A Stagecoach Approaching Dublin

Oil on panel

6 x 10 ins

15 x 25.5 cms

From the very early eighteenth century the favoured prospect of Dublin for artists was from its western approaches. Painters such as Thomas Bate and notably William Ashford (figure 46) charted the city's expansion along the Liffey and recorded the magnificent new public buildings built along its banks, most notably Kilmainham Hospital. This view was the subject of a series of works by Sadler which show a less grandly topographical and more intimate vision of the city. Although he painted purely topographical works such as the *View of Provost's House* (National Gallery of Ireland) Sadler is less concerned with buildings than with genre incident. In his *View of Dublin from the Phoenix Park* (private collection) (figure 47) he includes details such as smoke pouring from a chimney which would be quite out of place in the slightly idealised landscape of much the same subject by Ashford. Sadler is painting the Dublin of the new middle classes (his client base for small panels such as this) rather than the aristocratic capital of the eighteenth century. One of the artist's favourite motifs in these views is the horse drawn carriage which by the early nineteenth century had opened up the Irish midlands to more convenient reach from Dublin. In the view from Phoenix Park the carriage proceeds away from the city on its route west. In contrast in the present work its counterpart, carrying a mixture of soldiers and civilians, heads in towards Dublin. The view here is from slightly further away than Phoenix Park and the city is just visible on the horizon. In the foreground a rather unlikely genre scene shows two bathers, one swimming in a stream, one resting at its bank and an eagerly alert dog preparing to enter the water. Perhaps this is to suggest a sense of the contrast

Figure 46 William Ashford, *A View of Dublin from Chapelizod,*
reproduction courtesy of the National Gallery of Ireland

between the (supposed) world of rural ease and the busy city in the distance. As Brendan Rooney notes in his entry for Catalogue 16 the motif of bathers was to be taken up by Sadler's pupil James Arthur O'Connor. Interestingly it is also present as a background detail in van der Hagen's Kilsharvan House Capriccio (figure 13). This small landscape shows Sadler's technique at its finest. There is almost a *plein air* feeling in its directness. The artist uses great subtlety in his limited chromatic range. The darkness of the sides of the picture is enlivened by the burst of colour in the russet bush next to the seated bather. Dublin itself is enveloped in a flood of sunlight, a welcome prospect for the travellers coming to the end of their journey.

(W.L.)

Figure 47 Wiliam Sadler, *A View of Dublin from the Phoenix Park*, private collection

James Arthur O'Connor (1792 – 1841 (catalogue 15 – 17)

James Arthur O'Connor (figure 48) was born in 1792 in Dublin. It is reasonable to assume that he received some training from his father, William, a print-seller and engraver, but James Arthur did not pursue either of his father's professions. Instead, he took to landscape painting, a genre in which, it has been suggested, he may have received some direction from the Irish painter William Sadler (circa 1782 - 1839).[145] O'Connor exhibited first in 1809, at the Dublin Society,[146] and the following year at the Society of Artists of Ireland. Around two years later, he made the acquaintance of two other young and ambitious landscape painters, George Petrie (1790 - 1866) and Francis Danby (1793 - 1861). With them, O'Connor journeyed to London in 1813, where Petrie at least was presented to Benjamin West, former president of the Royal Academy. That introduction proved less auspicious than anticipated, and Petrie soon left for home. Shortly afterwards, O'Connor and Danby, having exhausted their funds, followed suit, and began their journey home via Bristol, where they arrived on foot. Having received a number of commissions there, Danby chose to stay, but O'Connor continued on to Dublin to look after his recently orphaned sisters. Despite his lack of success in London, and the general upheaval in his life, O'Connor managed to establish himself as a landscape painter in Dublin, exhibiting there regularly over subsequent years. He also received some prestigious and lucrative commissions, including a series of sixteen paintings of views around Westport, County Mayo and Portumna, County Galway, for the 2nd Marquis of Sligo and Lord Clonricarde. In 1818, O'Connor was also directly involved in the organization of the Exhibition of the Artists of Ireland in the Dublin Society's House,[147] and in 1821 received a premium of twenty-five guineas from the Royal Irish Institute. Such recognition and patronage could not keep O'Connor in

---

145 Strickland, Vol. 2, p. 179. O'Connor's name does not appear on the list of pupils at the Dublin Society Schools. See Gitta Willemson, (ed.), *The Dublin Society Drawing Schools. Students and Award Winners 1746 - 1876*, Dublin, 2000

146 Interestingly, the picture O'Connor contributed on that occasion was not a landscape, but entitled *Card players, a sketch*.

147 John Hutchinson, *James Arthur O'Connor*, exhibition catalogue, National Gallery of Ireland, Dublin, 1985, p. 89

Figure 48 After James Arthur O'Connor, *Self Portrait*, private collection

Ireland, however, and in 1821/2, 'in dismay and neglect, but not disgust',[148] he returned to London with his wife Anastatia, intent on exploiting broader opportunities. His work was accepted for exhibition at the Royal Academy for the first time in 1822, and on sixteen subsequent occasions up to 1840. He was also a regular exhibitor from 1829 at the Society of British Artists, of which he was elected a member, and the British Institution, where he showed thirty-eight pictures between 1823 and 1839. His exhibition pictures in England were exclusively landscapes, and many depicted Irish subjects.

In May 1826, O'Connor removed to Brussels with an art dealer by the name of Collier, or Collior, and remained there until the following year. Though the artist may have produced some commercially successful pictures during his sojourn on the continent, he was cheated out of money, possibly at the hands of his travelling companion. He returned to London, may have visited Ireland in 1828, and certainly did so in 1830. In September 1832, O'Connor, responding to his recurring *wanderlust*, left with Anastatia for Paris, where he stayed, painting with considerable success, until the following May. The couple intended continuing on to Italy, but on the advice and bogus promises of a stranger, opted instead to travel to the Saar and Moselle in south-west Germany. O'Connor was so enchanted by the landscape he encountered there that he abandoned his Italian tour altogether. Over the next six months, he travelled extensively in the region, and painted some of his finest works. On arrival back in London at the end of 1833, O'Connor, as before, resumed his profession with zeal, but now, notwithstanding the continuing acceptance of his work in exhibitions, with only moderate commercial success. His eyesight had begun to fail in 1833,[149] and in 1839, his general health fell into decline, as did his patronage. His consequent pecuniary difficulties were alleviated to some extent by Sir Charles Coote of Ballyfin, an enthusiastic patron of the arts, who commissioned a picture from O'Connor, and paid for it in advance. However, he remained in inextricable financial straits. He may have

---

148 'M', 'Memoirs of Native Artists, No. VII. James Arthur O'Connor', *The Citizen or Dublin Monthly Magazine*, April 1842, p. 260
149 Thomas Bodkin, *Four Irish Landscape Painters*, Dublin, 1920, p. 22

returned to Ireland in 1840 to paint a picture for Coote, as he exhibited for just the second time at the Royal Hibernian Academy that year.[150] He died at his home, No. 6 Marlborough Street, Brompton on 7th January 1841, leaving his wife destitute and ultimately dependent on the beneficence of the artist Martin Archer Shee and other colleagues.

O'Connor's legacy to Irish art is singular and impressive. Described by 'M' (probably George Mulvany) as 'generous in proclaiming contemporary merit, and unskilled and reluctant to put forth his own',[151] he appropriated essential qualities he had observed in English and continental art to his own work, but developed a style which also owed much to Irish artistic lineage. Anne Crookshank and the Knight of Glin have found echoes in O'Connor's oeuvre of the work of such disparate artists as Constable, Turner, Ruisdael, Georges Michel, and even Rembrandt,[152] and O'Connor also appears to owe a considerable debt to artists such as George Barret and the Roberts brothers, Thomas and Thomas Sautelle. O'Connor proved both accomplished and adaptable in his practice, producing a wide range of picture types, from topographical pictures (e.g. View of Westport with Croagh Patrick, 1818; Westport House), to picturesque rural scenes (e.g. A River Scene, Co. Wicklow, 1828; private collection), dramatic seascapes (A Sea Piece, 1839; private collection), romantic landscapes (The Poachers, 1835; National Gallery of Ireland), and hybrid curiosities (The Field at Waterloo, 1826; Anglesea Abbey Collection). He was also competent in etching, and in the use of pencil and watercolour.

---

150 O'Connor exhibited for the first time at the R.H.A. in 1830, with a painting entitled *The Glean of Oaks- A Storm Coming Up.*

151 'M', *op. cit.,* p. 266

152 Crookshank / Glin, 1978, p. 212

15.

James Arthur O'Connor

(1792 – 1841)

A Landscape with a View of Drimnagh Castle

Oil on canvas

17 ½ x 23 ½ ins

44.4 x 59.7 cms

signed and dated lower right: "JAO'Connnor 1821"

Provenance: Dr Cremin

Eamonn de Valera

Exhibited: *James Arthur O'Connor Centenary Exhibition,*

Hugh Lane Municipal Gallery, Dublin, 1941, no. 11,

incorrectly identified as *Roche's Castle, Ballyhooly, near Macroom*

O'Connor produced a number of works in response to a prevailing antiquarian interest in medieval architecture, such as views of Derry Castle, a ruin on the shores of Lough Derg (circa 1818); Tullow Church, County Dublin; and Bullock Castle, situated two miles east of Dun Laoghaire (1819).[153] He also painted medieval ruins during his sojourn on the Moselle, and executed an extensive view of Arundel Castle, Sussex (1824), a building which was substantially rebuilt and restored in the eighteenth century.[154]

Drimnagh Castle, situated off the Long Mile Road in south Dublin, was built around 1240, and served as the residence of the Anglo-Norman de Bernival (later Barnewall) family and their retinue. It was also 'a centre of administration for the whole area, including the lands of Terenure and Ballyfermot', and a formidable stronghold in times

---

153 Beranger produced topographical views of Bullock Castle as well.

154 For these subjects, see respectively *View of Lough Derg with Portumna Castle in the Background* (Westport House), *Bullock Castle and Bawn, County Dublin* (Gorry Gallery), *Tullow Church, Co. Dublin* (private collection) and *Arundel Castle* (Gorry Gallery).

Figure 49 William Brocas, *A View of Drimnagh Castle*, reproduction courtesy of the National Library of Ireland

of war.[155] William Brocas' sketch of the castle (figure 49), which is almost exactly contemporaneous with O'Connor's painting, gives a very clear impression of its raised location. In the eighteenth century it passed to the family of Arthur Archer, then to a Mr Reilly, and later still to the Hatch family, who presented it to the Irish Christian Brothers in 1954. When in the hands of the Barnewall family, the castle was lavishly appointed. Peter Harbison records that revenue from the family's vast tracts of land 'enabled them to furnish the interior in a more opulent style than most castle owners would have been able to afford'.[156] A comprehensive restoration of the castle was initiated in 1986 by the Drimnagh Castle Restoration Project under the auspices of An

155   Peter Pearson, 'Drimnagh Castle', in *Irish Arts Review*, Vol. 4, no. 2, Summer 1987, p. 50
156   Gabriel Beranger, *Drawings of the Principal Antique Buildings of Ireland*, Peter Harbison, (ed.), National Library of Ireland, Dublin, 1998, p. 42

Taisce and FÁS (the State Training and Employment agency).

The castle complex features a basic rectangular structure, consisting of a great hall over a vaulted undercroft, an adjoined three storey, sixteenth century gate tower, and a bawn. In the nineteenth century, after O'Connor painted his picture, a substantial coach house and stable block were added. The castle has the unusual distinction today of retaining its moat intact.[157] The stone bridge which leads up to the entrance in the painting was constructed in 1780 to replace the existing drawbridge,[158] while the large windows one can see in the upper storeys of the gate house are probably seventeenth century replacements of original, much narrower fenestration.

A View of Drimnagh Castle is notable for the manner in which an identified, and inhabited building is presented in relatively random surroundings. For a useful comparison, one can look at Beranger's neatly arranged, but topographically inaccurate drawings of the castle in 1760 (figure 50). This approach is in contrast to eighteenth century 'country house art', in which artists, including O'Connor, celebrated the houses and demesnes of the gentry in Britain and Ireland (see O'Connor's *Ballinrobe House, County Mayo* (circa 1770; National Gallery of Ireland) and *Westport House from Barratt's Hill* (1818; Westport House). Artists working in that idiom, adhering to a well-established model, were careful to impose order on their views of great houses and demesnes, or to faithfully represent the order inherent in their integrated landscapes. Drimnagh Castle, which was basically a medieval building in untamed grounds, did not lend itself to such formality. More importantly, however, the manner in which the castle is presented as part of, rather than dominating, the landscape, is consistent with O'Connor's general desire to celebrate in his pictures Nature's less predictable, romantic qualities. In this sense, *A View of Drimnagh Castle* afforded O'Connor the opportunity to indulge both his interest in topography, as seen in *A View of Irishtown from Sandymount*, and his interest in more ethereal, romantic

---

157   An underground stream called the Bluebell supplies the moat.
158   Pearson, *op. cit.,* p. 51

landscape, as expressed in *A Fisherman with his Catch on the Dargle.*

The detailing in this picture is typically deft and discerning. The waistcoat of the herdsman driving a cow and sheep across a bridge in the background, for instance, just a tiny speck of red, lifts the bluish green of the woodland further back, while the blue attire of the characteristically stiff figure to the right contrasts with the browns, greens and yellows of the castle and its surroundings. Elsewhere, the profile of a country church, faintly visible in the gap between the castle and the *repoussoir* trees to the left, enhances the authenticity of the scene, while the elegant presence of a swan on the moat adds to the serenity of the overall composition.

(B.R.)

Drumnagh Castle near Crumlin 2½ M. from DUBLIN. 1st View.

Figure 50 Gabriel Beranger, *Drimnagh Castle*, reproduction courtesy of the National Library of Ireland

16.

James Arthur O'Connor

(1792 – 1841)

A View of Irishtown from Sandymount

Oil on canvas

14 x 18 ins

35.5 x 45.7 cms

Signed and dated lower left: "JAO'Connor 1823"

Numerous diarists and travel writers of the eighteenth and nineteenth centuries wrote of Dublin Bay's pleasing aspect, some likening it to the bay of Naples. A very large number of pictures of Dublin Bay, both by artists resident in Ireland and others visiting from abroad, corroborate these descriptions,[159] but also constitute a fascinating visual history of the development of Ireland's capital and its commercial port. Artists of the eighteenth and nineteenth centuries, such as Francis Place (1647 -1728), William Jones (*fl*. 1744 - 47), William Ashford (1746 - 1824), Christopher Machell (1747 - 1827), John Henry Campbell (1755 - 1828), Thomas Sautell Roberts (1760 - 1826), William Sadler (1782 - 1839), Francis Danby (1793 - 1861) (figure 51) and William Craig (1829 - 75), working in a variety of media, produced both panoramic views of the bay and scenes of specific locations along its north and south shores.

O'Connor's painting presents a view of Irishtown, an old village just outside the city, from below Scald Hill, near Sandymount. In the centre of the composition stands a wooden hut, possibly used by local fishermen or as shelter for swimmers, while edging into the picture on the left is the gable end of one of the buildings of a baths complex. In the background one can see the South Wall, and in the extreme distance the low hills of Clontarf and Raheny on the north side of the bay.

The building of the North and South Walls in Dublin bay, undertaken by the newly

---

159   Gabrielle Ricciardelli (fl. 1745 - 77) painted the ports of Dublin, Naples and Valetta in a similar vein.

Figure 51 Francis Danby, *Ringsend from Beggar's Bush*, reproduction courtesy of the National Gallery of Ireland

established Ballast Office shortly after 1707, represented one of the most ambitious engineering projects of the eighteenth century in Ireland.[160] The construction of the walls was carried out in stages, and though by the middle of the century the main construction was virtually complete, development continued into the nineteenth century. While the North Wall projected just over a mile from the old mouth of the River Liffey, the South Wall extended over four miles into the bay. Prominent features along its length by the end of the eighteenth century were the alarmingly

160   Maurice Craig, *Dublin 1660 - 1860*, Dublin, 1969, p. 90

Figure 52 James Arthur O'Connor, *A View of Irishtown from Sandymount*,
courtesy of the Huntington Library, Art Collections, and Botanical Gardens, San Marino, California.

Figure 53 John Henry Campbell, *Ringsend and Irishtown from the Grand Canal*,
reproduction courtesy of the National Gallery of Ireland

exposed Pigeon House watch-house and hostelry (circa 1766),[161] its adjacent basin and military barracks (1791 - 95),[162] which were painted a number of times by William Sadler in the early years of the nineteenth century (see figure 45), and the lighthouse (later called the Poolbeg lighthouse, completed in 1767), which terminated it.[163]

---

161   H.A. Gilligan, *A History of the Port of Dublin*, Dublin, 1988, p. 38
162   The barracks were originally built as a hostel, but in 1798 were commandeered by the Lord Lieutenant for the army in response to domestic unrest and the threat of French invasion. Gilligan, *op. cit.*, p. 61
163   The Pigeon House derived its name from its first proprietor, John Pigeon, an employee of the Ballast Office.

A pen and ink drawing by O'Connor of exactly the same subject (figure 52), which is clearly a preparatory sketch for the oil painting, provides an insight into the artist's approach to landscape, as there are significant differences in detail between the two pictures. The immediacy and summary nature of the drawing suggest that it was either executed *sur le motif*, or was at least a literal representation of a scene observed. In one sense, then, it can be taken as a more authentic representation of the scene than the oil painting. Typically, the painting appears to be an altogether more refined, highly finished piece, certainly based on drawings, but embellished considerably to enhance the picturesque quality of the scene. Though the viewpoint appears to be identical in the two pictures, the bell tower of St Matthew's Church, Irishtown, which adds interest to the roofline in this painting, and many others of the village, is conspicuously absent from the drawing. It seems likely that O'Connor introduced this landmark, which would have been hidden behind the gable of the building on the extreme left, not simply to improve the painting compositionally, but also to identify the location. St Matthew's was synonymous with Irishtown, and is clearly visible in views of the village by Jones (Private collection),[164] Ricciardelli (National Gallery of Ireland), Ashford (National Gallery of Ireland) and Campbell (National Gallery of Ireland) (figure 53). In A. Neville's revised map of 'Part of the Estate of the Rt Honble the Earl of Pembroke & Montgomery' of 1826[165] Irishtown is denoted simply by a representation of the church. According to Elrington Ball, the Royal Chapel of St Matthew, commonly known as Irishtown Church, was originally erected because flooding from rain and high tides often made it impossible for local people to attend the nearby parish church of Donnybrook.[166] Also absent from O'Connor's drawing, but clearly visible in the mid distance on the right of the painting, is a sloping gangway on the South Wall, along which a line of passengers queues. From the seventeenth to

164 In the context of the development of the bay, it is interesting to note that the North Wall with the North Wall House is clearly visible in Giles King's engraving of 1745 after Jones' view of the Dublin Bay, but is absent from the original painting.

165 'Part of the Estate of the Rt Honble the Earl of Pembroke & Montgomery/ Surveyed by John Roe/ Revised by A. Neville Jun. 14 York Street 1826'. National Archives, Dublin, 97/46/4/17. The author is greatly indebted to Eve McAulay, who is currently completing a doctorate on the development of the Pembroke Estate, for furnishing him with primary information.

166 Francis Elrington Ball, *A History of the County Dublin*, Vol. II, Dublin, 1903, p. 39

the nineteenth century, before the development of the harbours at Howth and Kingstown, Ringsend was the 'chief place of embarkation and disembarkation for passenger traffic'.[167] This included not just traffic to and from the sea, but also passengers to and from Dublin, who were ferried to the Pigeon House from Ringsend.[168] The inclusion of the line of figures, though extremely understated, also

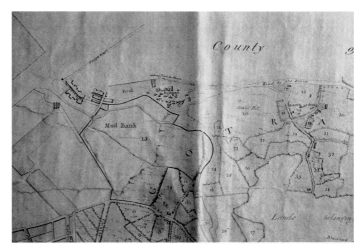

Figure 54 John Roe, *A Map of the Fitzwilliam Estate between Merrion Square and Blackrock*, (1794), National Archives, Dublin

afforded O'Connor the opportunity to introduce extra colour into the scene, thus enlivening the whole composition. Such abrogation of topographical accuracy in the interests of character and visual harmony is consistent with O'Connor's general interests in the compositional and romantic potential of scenes observed.

John Roe's map of 1794, on which Neville's was based, of that part of Lord Viscount Fitzwilliam's estate between Merrion Square and Blackrock (figure 54),[169] allows one to identify the areas encompassed by O'Connor's scene. Though the map was produced some twenty-five years before O'Connor's painting, the profile of the bay and its constituent elements remained relatively unchanged over the intervening decades. One can clearly see the small scattering of buildings that made up Irishtown, and the adjacent village of Ringsend, which abutted the South Wall. These small fishing

167 *Ibid.*, p. 35
168 See Gilligan, *op. cit.*, pp. 57 - 59
169 'A Map of that Part of the Estate of the Rt. Honble Richard Lord Visct. Fitzwilliam between the Merrion Square and the Blackrock particularly describing the Lane which separates the County from the County of the City of Dublin by John Roe 1794', National Archives, Dublin, 2011/2/1/40

villages nestled between the bay to the north and a combination of slob-land, mud flats, and undeveloped pasture to the south. As the Pembroke (formerly Fitzwilliam) Estate was developed during the nineteenth century, the land around Ringsend and Irishtown was drained and built upon, so that these villages were gradually surrounded by the expanding metropolis.

O'Connor painted his picture, therefore, at a very significant time in the development of the bay and the areas that flanked it. The North and South Walls were now well-established features of the bay, and the residential districts of north and south Dublin were reaching out eastwards. The Ringsend Docks, the opening ceremony of which was recorded in admirable detail by William Ashford (1796; National Gallery of Ireland), provided direct access to the bay from the Grand Canal, which itself connected the east coast to the midlands. Dublin was a flourishing port for both commercial and passenger vessels, and was perpetually occupied by tall ships, many of which had to drop anchor in the open bay until tide levels allowed them to make the journey into the city. Air travel, the modern development of the North Wall Port and the passenger port of Dun Laoghaire (formerly Kingstown) has meant that it is now difficult to appreciate the volume of traffic that Dublin Bay received at this time, and its fundamental importance to the economy.

However, O'Connor, by including the masts of tall ships at anchor, or travelling in or out of port behind the South Wall in the distance, makes only oblique reference here to Dublin as a mercantile capital. The wall serves as a monument to engineering and a flourishing city, but perhaps more importantly as a demarcation line between the city and the small villages on its fringes. Ringsend and Irishtown were quite independent from Dublin, and indeed, from each other, though they stood cheek-by-jowl. Moreover, though recorded as reasonably prosperous at the beginning of the eighteenth century, by the 1820s they were far from affluent.

Richard Mathew, Lord Fitzwilliam's agent, was reasonably positive about the potential of Irishtown in the middle of the eighteenth century, writing to his employer that "The poor inhabitants are mostly Widdows, whose Husbands being Fisher Men, have been pressd and perished, in the Service, or Strayd abroade, you woude be Surprized to See, In what a decent manner they have dressd up theire Little Houses, and have Reason to belive this Place will rise (If Encouraged) and In some measure make Amends, for the Ruines at Ringsend."[170] His optimism appears somewhat misplaced, however, as Barbara Verschoyle, who occupied the same position almost sixty years later, stated with alarming, patrician invective in 1801 that she had taken it upon herself to introduce 'a little degree of cleanlyness and decency' to Ringsend and Irishtown. The people of Irishtown, she maintained, were 'wretchedly poor- & ever must be so- while they are so idle- I had no idea they were half so bad- until I went through their Cabins- when I enquired for the men I was told they were at Sea (for they are all most all fishermen) & to the Women I said what do you do- have you any way to earn bread- do you spin- do you knit- No- we gather cockels the young ones replied- the Old hawked the fish the men caught- in short it was quite shocking'.[171] Verschoyle then assured her employer that she would endeavour to replace any evicted leaseholders with 'improving tenants'.[170] She may have had in mind the likes of William Ashford, for whom Gandon had designed a villa in Sandymount in the late 1780s.[173]

Verschoyle's assessment of the area was repeated just a few years before O'Connor painted his scene, by Warburton, Whitelaw and Walsh, who remarked that 'when a stranger, after contemplating the delightful scenery of the bay, enters the river, in his ascent to the city, the objects that immediately surround him are calculated to excite disappointment and disgust: on the left, after he had passed the wretched village of

170   Letter from Richard Mathew to Lord Fitzwilliam, Dublin, 27th August 1747, *Pembroke Correspondences*, National Archives, Dublin, 97.46.1.2.5.46
171   Letter from Barbara Verschoyle to Lord Fitzwilliam, 5th April 1801, *Pembroke Estate Letter Book*, Vol. I, National Archives, Dublin.
172   *Ibid.*
173   The site for Ashford's house corresponds to plot number 28 on Roe's map of 1794.

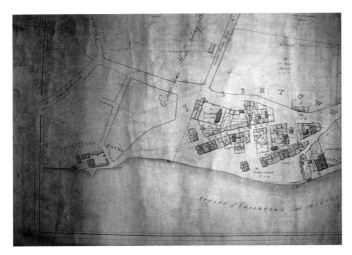

Figure 55 Sherrard, Brassington and Gale, *Survey of Ringsend and Irishtown,* (1830), National Archives, Dublin

Ringsend, consisting of a few ruinous houses.....on either hand he has the north and south walls, which here have a ruinous aspect...'.[174]

Despite the poverty, Ringsend and Irishtown were renowned for good pickings of cockles and shrimp, and also drew the citizens of Dublin for occasional horse racing and, as mentioned above, bathing. The structure on the extreme left of O'Connor's painting is part of the complex known as 'Cranfield's Baths', clearly visible on Sherrard, Brassington and Gale's map of 1830 (figure 55),[175] which was established after 1797 by Richard Cranfield (1731-1809), the carver.[176] With a person by the name of Rogers, he held the lease for the plot on which these baths stood, and had interests in land elsewhere in the area.[177] Though these baths used water from the bay, they were self-contained, private, and effectively inaccessible to the local impoverished population. The perceived benefits of bathing in sea water led to the establishment of a number of baths in Dublin during this period.[178] As early as 1747, Richard Mathew stated that 'The Cittizens of Dublin have as I hinted sometime passd taken an Humour (I cant tell how long it will hold) To Vissite Irishtowne, and for this Season, all the little Cabbins

---

174   J. Warburton, Rev. J. Whitelaw, Robert Walsh, *History of the City of Dublin,* Vol. 2, London, 1818, p. 441

175   'Survey of Ringsend & Irishtown in the County of Dublin Part of the Estate of The Honble. Sidney Herbert By Sherrard, Brassington and Gale', National Archives, Dublin, 2011/2/1. This map allows one to identify with considerable accuracy the viewpoint for O'Connor's scene.

176   Strickland, Vol. 1, p. 219

177   The plot in question corresponds to no. 78 on Neville's map. Cranfield also held the lease for plot no. 81 in Sandymount from the same map. The leases remained in his name after his death until at least 1830.

178   These included Murphy's Baths in Irishtown, also marked on Sherrard, Brassington and Gale's map.

are hired by Lodgers, to have the Advantage of Bathing in the Salt Watter…'.[179] Other bathing huts, marked on Roe's map, and John Roque's famous map of 1756, as being 'for women', could be found immediately adjacent to the village of Irishtown.

The characters, two in their undershirts, who rest and talk in the shadow of the wooden hut in O'Connor's painting, are most likely locals. Their clothes do not suggest particular affluence, and their behaviour is at odds with prevailing etiquette among the higher echelons of society.[180] Admittedly, women were more subject to social constraint, but the activity of the men in this picture is particularly casual and public. Moreover, during the same period, O'Connor painted very comparable pictures of working class men bathing in the sea at Seapoint, near Kingstown (1820; private collection) and near Duffy's Cotton Mills, Ballsbridge (circa 1818 - 20; private collection).

As John Hutchinson has pointed out, pictures such as these, quite different to O'Connor's earlier 'house portraits', were middle class in their appeal.[181] They occupy a category between genre painting and topographical landscape, recording not just the physical nature of the scene, but also the prosaic activity of its visitors and inhabitants. Significantly, however, these pictures do not provide any indication of the quotidian hardship, referred to by the above writers, endured by the city's poor.

(B.R.)

---

179   Letter from Richard Mathew to Lord Fitzwilliam, *op. cit.*

180   The figures in O'Connor's preparatory drawing, labourers rather than bathers, also appear in peasant attire.

181   John Hutchinson, *James Arthur O'Connor*, exhibition catalogue, National Gallery of Ireland, Dublin, 1985, p. 120

17.

James Arthur O'Connor

(1792 – 1841)

A Dargle Landscape with a Fisherman

Oil on canvas

13 ½ x 18 ins

34 x 46 cms

Signed lower left: "JAO'Connor"

Provenance: Dr Cremin

Eamonn de Valera

Like Dublin Bay, the River Dargle attracted the attention of a number of artists throughout the eighteenth and nineteenth centuries, among them George Barret, Thomas Roberts (1748 - 78), Thomas Walmsley (1763 - 1806) and Daniel Maclise (1806 - 70). It was presented in various forms, from grand, monumental scenes, to topographical sketches and intimate landscapes.

The Dargle river develops from the confluence of the Glenislorane and Glencree rivers which flow from Lough Bray, and becomes the Bray river which meets the sea at the town of Bray, County Wicklow. Artists were struck by the picturesque quality of the Dargle, and particularly its renowned Lovers' Leap.[182] George Barret's paintings of Powerscourt may have been the first indigenous Irish landscapes to have been exhibited in London,[183] and helped to establish Irish landscape painting there as a separate category within the genre. Irish subjects, such as the Dargle, and the skill with which they were recorded by particularly talented individuals, allowed Irish artists to present themselves in England not simply as provincial figures, but as painters with a distinct vision, yet on a par with their English contemporaries.

---

182   James Arthur O'Connor painted both the Lovers' Leap and the waterfall at Powerscourt.
183   Fintan Cullen, *Visual Politics: The Representation of Ireland 1750 - 1930*, Cork, 1997, p. 15

Figure 56 James Arthur O'Connor, *A Fisherman by the Dargle,* private collection

This is one of a series of related works that O'Connor painted during his career (see figure 56). It lacks the documentary quality which adds such interest now to pictures like *A View of Irishtown from Sandymount* and *A View of Drimnagh Castle*, but nevertheless is as indicative of its time as it is of its creator, and is typically accomplished in execution. O'Connor, recalled Mulvany in *The*

Figure 57 George Barret, *A Landscape with Fishermen*,
reproduction courtesy of the National Gallery of Ireland

Dublin Monthly Magazine, loved the Dargle. 'Its quiet retirement', he said, 'its picturesque intricacies, its moss-covered rocks at once entranced the painter and pleased the man….. Jarring, flaunting, noisy bustle, were out of keeping with the quiet peace of his heart'.[184] These works follow very closely the tradition of views of the Irish landscape established by George Barret (1728 or 1732 - 87), not just thematically, but also in the tone of the paintings and in their distinctly Irish character (figure 57). In his youth, Barret came under the powerful influence of his near contemporary Edmund Burke, who expressed his theories on aesthetics in his seminal *Philosophical Enquiry into the Origins of our Ideas of the Sublime and the Beautiful*, published in 1757.[185] Burke, who identified the Sublime as those qualities in nature which inspire awe, terror or feelings of solitude in the viewer, and the Beautiful as those alternative qualities which evoke feelings of tranquillity, serenity and repose, encouraged Barret

---

184   'M', 'Memoirs of Native Artists, No. VII, James Arthur O'Connor', in *The Citizen* or *Dublin Monthly Magazine*, April 1842, p. 260
185   For Burke see the essay by Patrick Healy above.

to study directly from Nature rather than copy from Old Masters and antique sources. Barret's application of Burke's advice was facilitated by the patronage of the 2nd Viscount Powerscourt, in whose vast and impressive demesne in Wicklow Barret produced a number of splendid pictures. Among these were scenes of the Dargle river.

Many of Barret's landscapes possess an atmospheric grandeur which transcended Burke's direction. Moreover, they were invariably deliberate 'compositions', rather than unmediated empirical observations, or simply the work of 'a wonderful observer of the accidents of nature' as Barret was described by Burke himself.[186] Though George Barret juxtaposed diminutive figures with vast, overwhelming natural features in some of his pictures, including *A View of Powerscourt Waterfall* (National Gallery of Ireland) he did not necessarily adhere as rigidly to Burke's notion of the Sublime as this alone would suggest. John Hutchinson has reasonably suggested that on occasion Barret modified Burke's theories through the introduction of elements such as the 'golden sky in the background'.[187] Many of James Arthur O'Connor's Wicklow views appear to have been informed by this aesthetic, as well as Thomas Roberts' more delicate and exacting approach to Irish subjects (see, for example, Roberts' views of Lucan demesne (National Gallery of Ireland), Clonskeagh Bridge (Private collection) and Slane Castle (Private collection).[188] Though painted later than Roberts' prospects, O'Connor's views are similarly evocative, focusing on the grand, picturesque and romantic qualities of indigenous Irish landscape.

---

186   James Barry, *The Works of James Barry*, (Edward Fryer (ed.)), Vol. 1, London, 1809, p. 89
187   John Hutchinson, *James Arthur O'Connor*, exhibition catalogue, National Gallery of Ireland, Dublin, 1985, p. 83
188   The crispness with which O'Connor delineates foliage, ideally suited to his smaller scale compositions, is much more reminiscent of Thomas Roberts' work than Barret's.

O'Connor had a healthy complement of that ability to identify and disseminate the innate qualities in Nature which was so characteristic of Barret. As Mulvany succinctly expressed it, 'the deep and darkly wooded glen; the grey, weather-bleached, massive rock, crowned with the stunted oak or sparkling holly, hanging o'er the rushing waters; or the moss-covered trunk of gnarled oak, draped with the clinging ivy, standing as though he guarded the narrow mountain pass, where the jaded traveller is seen, wending his lonely way towards yon distant column of deep blue smoke- these were the subjects [O'Connor] delighted to paint, and into which he poured the whole feeling of his soul'.[189] O'Connor's own testimony demonstrates the perspicacity of Mulvany's observations. 'I am going to the wild and beautiful scenery of my native country to refresh my memory', O'Connor wrote to John Gibbons in August 1830. 'I know', he went on, 'that I will be benefited by a sight of the grand... scenery I will meet with in Ireland, and hope to show it on canvas'.[190]

It is interesting to note that O'Connor neglected to animate the small figures which populate the majority of his works. More often than not, they stand stock still,[191] as if petrified by the artist's gaze. In this way, they curiously pre-empt early formal photography, in which human subjects, who were *required* to stand still, appear rigid and uncomfortable. In *A Fisherman with his Catch on the Dargle*, the figure stands facing the viewer, holding his catch by his side with one hand, and his rod equally stiffly in the other. Inexpressive and inactive, he is essentially an adjunct to the landscape. As Thomas Bodkin pointed out, O'Connor's introduction into his landscapes of 'a little figure in a red coat or wearing a red cap' was 'a device of contrast' which lent his greens greater value and brilliancy',[192] but here, the figure serves other functions as well. His diminutive size emphasises the density and scale

---

189   'M', *op. cit.*, p. 265
190   Quoted in Hutchinson, *op. cit.*, p. 151
191   For alternative examples see *Homeward Bound* (circa 1825 - 30; National Gallery of Ireland), *Wooded River Landscape with Figures* (circa 1830; Gorry Gallery), *Rhine Landscape* (circa 1833; Ulster Museum), *Landscape: Sunset after Rain* (1838; Gorry Gallery) and *Coastal Landscape with a Figure on a Path* (1838; private collection).
192   Bodkin, *op. cit.*, p. 25

of the surrounding landscape, while the relative success of his endeavours (i.e. his catch), communicates the river's lively, fertile and unspoilt quality. The fact that O'Connor did occasionally animate his figures (see, for example, some of his etchings in the British Museum and larger works such as *The Nut Gatherers* (Private collection) and *A Thunderstorm: The Frightened Wagoner* (National Gallery of Ireland)), suggests that the relative inertia one often sees in them was deliberate. *A Fisherman with his Catch on the Dargle* is a serene image, but features touches of the bold brushwork and thick application of paint which distinguish some of O'Connor's more dramatic landscapes.

(B.R.)

18.

Peter Turnerelli
(1774 – 1839)

A Head and Shoulders Portrait Bust of Henry Grattan (1746 – 1820)
White marble on its original carved socle
Height 23 ins; 58.5 cms
signed and dated on the reverse: "P. Turnerelli Sculpt 1820" see figure 58
Literature: Walter Strickland, *A Dictionary of Irish Artists,*
Dublin, 1913, (1969), Vol. 2, p. 467 and 469
Anne Crookshank and The Knight of Glin, *Irish Portraits, 1660 – 1860,*
London, 1969, p. 87
Richard Walker, *National Portrait Gallery, Regency Portraits,*
London, 1985, Vol. 1, p. 223 and Vol. 2, no. 516

The present marble bust is one of the masterpieces of Irish neo-classical sculpture. It is perhaps Turnerelli's finest work and depicts one of the greatest statesmen and orators of eighteenth-century Ireland. Indeed Turnerelli's depiction of Grattan was praised by none other than Canova, the greatest of all neo-classical sculptors and friend of Hugh Douglas Hamilton (see figure 29). Seeing it in the artist's studio he was "particularly attracted to it" and described it as "the best modern bust I have seen in England".[193] The present version of the bust was executed in the year of Grattan's death two decades after the Act of Union had brought an end to Irish independence, the cause to which Grattan devoted his life.

Henry Grattan (figure 59) was born in Dublin in 1746. His father James was an M.P. and Recorder of Dublin while his mother Mary was the daughter of Thomas Marlay, Chief Justice of Ireland. At Trinity College he immersed himself in the study and translation of classical rhetoric and in 1775 was elected to Parliament with the help of

---

193 *European Magazine,* May 1821, p. 389

Figure 58 Detail of signature of catalogue 18

Lord Charlemont. His impact on the Irish House of Commons was immediate. His character and oratory made him the natural leader of the Patriotic party. Compared by Byron to Demosthenes, Grattan's style of rhetoric was well described by Lecky. "His thoughts naturally crystallised into epigrams; his arguments were condensed with such admirable force and clearness that they assumed almost the appearance of axioms; and they were often interspersed with sentences of concentrated poetic beauty, which flashed upon the audience with all the force of sudden inspiration, and which were long remembered and repeated."[194] Grattan spoke out against the corruption of absentee placemen with government sinecures and the malign influence of Dublin Castle on Irish life. In October 1779 he moved an amendment declaring that the only effective remedy for the existing distress of Ireland was to "open its ports for exportation of its manufactures" – a Free Trade principal to which political self-determination was the next logical step. He followed this up with campaigns for limiting taxes voted by Westminster without the consent of the Irish parliament. On 19th April 1780, in a debate on the repeal of Poynings Law, he proposed the motion "that the people of Ireland are of right an independent nation and ought only to be bound by the laws made by the King, Lords and Commons of Ireland". The debate lasted fifteen hours but the vote was adjourned. This historic occasion was captured by Francis Wheatley an English artist then visiting Dublin who was given special access to the chamber (figure 60).

Largely through the advocacy of Grattan's rhetoric the Irish parliament gained a degree

---

194   William Lecky, *The Leaders of Public Opinion in Ireland*, London, 1871, p. 109

of independence it had not enjoyed for centuries. He summed up its achievements. "Of that assembly I have a parental recollection. I sat by her cradle, I followed her hearse. In fourteen years she achieved for Ireland what you in England did not achieve in a century; freedom of trade, independence of the legislature, independence of the judges, restoration of the final judicature, repeal of a perpetual mutiny bill, a Habeas Corpus Act...." Indeed Grattan's parliament saw a period of wealth unparalleled in Ireland - until the present day. In the ten years from 1782 exports more than trebled and, as one

Figure 59 F. Gallé, *Portrait Medal of Henry Grattan,* (private collection)

commentator noted at the time, in words strangely familiar to modern Ireland, "there is not a nation in the habitable globe which has advanced in cultivation and commerce...with the same rapidity".[195] However in 1800, the Act of Union, forced through by bribery, brought an end to Grattan's dreams, although he carried on campaigning for his ideals. He died in London in 1820 having set off in ill health to address the Westminster parliament on behalf of his constituents.

The remarkable quality of much eighteenth and early nineteenth century Irish sculpture is still little appreciated. The outstanding contribution that Irish sculptors made to the neo-classical movement was, however, acknowledged at the time. *The Art Journal* for August 1861, for example noted: "Ireland has contributed to the British School of Art more good sculptors – indeed many of our best – than she has painters....; we can not account for the fact, but know such is the case and could

---

195   Quoted *ibid.,* p. 189

181

Figure 60 Francis Wheatley, *Henry Grattan Addressing the Irish House of Commons*, Leeds Museums and Galleries
(Lotherton Hall) U.K / Bridgeman Art Library

prove it, if necessary, by indisputable evidence."[196] While the greatest Irish sculptor of the eighteenth century, Christopher Hewetson, spent almost his entire career in Italy, the process was reversed with the Turnerelli family. Giacomo Tognarelli an Italian refugee spent most of his life in Ireland working as a sculptor in Belfast until 1787 when he moved to Dublin. His son Peter (figure 61) who anglicised the family name was born in Belfast and initially trained for the Church at a seminary in Meath, a plan

---

196   Quoted in Anne Crookshank and the Knight of Glin, *Irish Portraits 1660 – 1860*, London, 1969, p. 83

abandoned when the family moved to London in 1792, where Turnerelli enrolled in the Royal Academy Schools, also studying with Peter Chenu. He excelled as a student and in 1799 won the Academy's silver medal for sculpture. Early commissions included busts of Sir Francis Drake and General Eliot for Lord Heathfield. Sir Thomas Lawrence, President of the Royal Academy recommended him to the Princess of Wales who engaged him as a teacher of modelling. After three years he was appointed Royal Sculptor-in-Ordinary and was offered a knighthood which, however, he declined. Turnerelli showed at the Royal Academy for the first time in 1802 when his exhibits included *A Nest of Cupids* and *Bust of the Rev. Arthur O'Leary* and he was a regular exhibitor until the years before his death. In 1810 he received the commission for the Jubilee bust of George III which was such an instantaneous success that he received orders for eighty copies of it in marble from the nobility of England and various colonies. The following year he exhibited a statue of the King in his robes of state.

International success soon followed. He was appointed sculptor to the Emperor of Russia and to the Kings of France and Portugal. He executed busts of, among others, The Duke of Wellington, Field Marshall Blucher, Prince Leopold and the Duke of Cumberland. However, Turnerelli frequently found time to return to Ireland working on the High Altar for the Pro-Cathedral in Dublin and executing a monument to Bishop Moynan in Cork. In 1813 at the instance of Lord Kinnaird he visited Grattan at his country estate at Tinnahinch where "he modelled the bust of that celebrated orator in 11 hours. The bust was esteemed by every person who knew Mr Grattan, as a truly classical specimen of sculpture art, which they considered as a faithful likeness, or as a bold and animated picture of the mind and intellectual character of that distinguished patriot."[197] This bust was exhibited at the Royal Academy in 1812 and is still in the possession of the family of Lord Kinnaird at Rossie Priory while a marble replica was formerly at Adare Manor.[198] The present bust is of a slightly different type which Turnerelli produced to mark the death of Grattan in 1820. A version of this is

197 *European Magazine, op. cit.*
198 Richard Walker, *National Portrait Gallery, Regency Portraits*, London, 1985, Vol. 1, p. 223

appropriately housed in the Bank of Ireland in Dublin, before the Act of Union the Irish Houses of Parliament, scene to his greatest triumphs. Although the face is almost identical the 1820 version differs from the 1812 bust by its inclusion of a toga. Paradoxically Turnerelli was (at the suggestion of Benjamin West) the first Irish sculptor to show his sitters in contemporary dress rather than in the stylised classical drapery which had become conventional. Here, however, it is wholly appropriate that the great orator should be attired in the manner of a Roman senator. Turnerelli also produced a bust of the next great figure in Irish nationalist history Daniel O'Connell which met with great public success – no fewer than 10,000 plaster copies of it were sold.

Turnerelli's status at Ireland's premier sculptor of the first half of the nineteenth century is indisputable. His work has a direct vigour, truthfulness and presence which sets him apart from the dull, attenuated pomp that typifies so much portrait sculpture of the period. Even when his subjects are clad in stylised Roman dress they have an immediacy, indeed intimacy, which bears witness to his psychological understanding and technical mastery. None of the many portraits of Grattan by artists such as Shee and Stuart or indeed the famous statue by John Foley in College Green does as much justice to his complex character "a fascinating mixture of vehemence and benevolence".[199] The international neo-classical style in which Irish artists such as Robert Fagan and Hugh Douglas Hamilton had flourished while working in Italy is here triumphantly brought home to Ireland.

(W.L.)

197   *European Magazine, op. cit.*
198   Richard Walker, *National Portrait Gallery, Regency Portraits*, London, 1985, Vol. 1, p. 223
199   Lecky, *op. cit.*, p. 152

Figure 61 J. Thomson after S. Drummond, *Portrait of Peter Turnerelli, European Magazine,*
   May 1821

INDEX OF ARTISTS

BIBLIOGRAPHY OF CATALOGUES
Published by Pyms Gallery 1980 - 2001

YEAR: TITLE AND AUTHOR

1980   E.H.H. Archibald, Foreword, *19th and early 20th Century Marine and Coastal Paintings and Watercolours,* London, April 1980

1981   Mary Hobart, *Marine and Coastal Paintings and Watercolours of the 19th and early 20th Century,* London, April 1981

1981   Bruce Arnold, *William Orpen - Early Work,* London, May 1981

1981   Mary Hobart, *Marine and Coastal Paintings and Watercolours of the 19th and Early 20th Century,* London, April 1981

1981   Kenneth McConkey, Foreword, *Edwardian Impressions - An Exhibition of Late Nineteenth and Early Twentieth Century Paintings,* London, October 1981

1982   Mary Hobart, Foreword by Bruce Arnold, *The Irish Revival,* London, May 1982

1982   Janet Barnes, *Percy Horton, Artist and Absolutist 1897 - 1970,* Sheffield, September 1982, in association with Graves Art Gallery, Newcastle Polytechnic Gallery and City Museum and Art Gallery, Stoke-on-Trent.

1983   Mary Hobart, Annette Wilson, *William James Yule (1867 - 1900), A Scottish Impressionist,* London, April 1983

1983   Bruce Arnold, Kenneth McConkey, G.P. Weisberg et al., *Autumn Anthology - An Exhibition of British French and Irish Paintings,* London, October 1983.

1984   Mary Hobart, Annette Wilson, *Charles Oakley's Trompe L'Oeil Tableaux, Works with Romantic and Historical Associations,* London, March 1984

1984   Kenneth McConkey, Caroline Fox, Gabriel Weisberg et al, *Rural and Urban Images - An Exhibition of British and French Paintings 1870 - 1920,* London, October 1984

1985   Kenneth McConkey et al., *Impressions and Realities - An Exhibition of British, French and Irish Paintings, 1850 - 1930,* London, November 1985

1985   Kenneth McConkey, Essay. Catalogue Entries by McConkey, Jonathan Benington et al., *Celtic Splendour - An Exhibition of Irish Paintings and Drawings,* London, April 1985

1986   Kenneth McConkey et al., *Lost Illusions, Works with Romantic and Historical Associations by Charles Oakley,* London, March 1986, in association with the Arts Council of Northern Ireland

1986   Julian Campbell, *Paintings by Mary Swanzy, H.R.H.A. (1882 - 1978),* London, September 1986

1986	Kenneth McConkey, Essay. Catalogue Entries by McConkey, Jonathan Benington et al., *Irish Renascence - Irish Art in a Century of Change*. London, November 1986
1987	Kenneth McConkey et al., *Orpen and the Edwardian Era*, London, November 1987
1988	Andrew George et al., *Mentors and Mementoes, an Exhibition of Works with Romantic and Historical Associations by Charles Oakley*, London, September 1988, supported by Northern Arts.
1989	Fionnuala Brennan, *Mary Swanzy, H.R.H.A. (1882 - 1978)*, London, November 1989
1990	Kenneth McConkey, *A Free Spirit - Irish Art 1860 - 1960*, joint publication with The Antique Collectors Club, London, June 1990
1991	Kenneth McConkey et al., *Life and Landscape - in French, British and Irish Painting at the Turn of the Century*. London, May 1991
1991	Kenneth McConkey et al., *Orpen at Howth*, London, June 1991
1993	Jonathan Benington, McConkey, et al., *An Ireland Imagined, Irish Paintings and Drawings 1860 - 1960*, London, 1993
1995	John Hayes, *The Holloway Gainsborough*, London, 1995
1996	Kenneth McConkey, Essay, *Truth to Nature – French, British and Irish Painting of the Nineteenth and Twentieth Centuries*, London, 1996
1998	Mary and Alan Hobart, *An Exhibition of Paintings by Mary Swanzy H.R.H.A. (1882 - 1978)*, London, May 1998
1998	Kenneth McConkey, *John Singer Sargent's A Spanish Woman (Gigia Viani)*, London, November 1998
1998	Andrew George, *Edwardian Impressionist - The Art of Harry Mitton Wilson (1887 - 1923)*, London, December 1998
1999	Anne Crookshank, The Knight of Glin, William Laffan, *Masterpieces by Irish Artists (1660 - 1860)*, London, June 1999
1999	Kenneth McConkey, introduction by Hector McDonnell, *Live Eels and Juicy Fruits - City Scenes and Interiors by Hector McDonnell*, London, November 1999.
2000	Sarah Wilson, *Colin Watson, Paintings of Mood and Place*, London, May 2000
2000	William Laffan, *Robert Fagan in Sicily - The Acton Family Portrait*, London, June 2000
2000	Kenneth McConkey, *Edwardian Pre-Raphaelites - The Art of John and Mary Young Hunter*, London, June 2000
2001	Anne Crookshank, The Knight of Glin, Nicola Figgis, Brendan Rooney, Patrick Healy, (ed. William Laffan), *The Sublime and the Beautiful - Irish Art 1700 - 1830*. London, June 2001

Pyms Gallery was established in 1975. From its inception its founders, Alan and Mary Hobart have set exacting standards in the research, presentation and intrinsic quality of the works of art that have passed through their hands. They have been widely recognized as specialists in the field of eighteenth, nineteenth and early twentieth century British and French paintings and all periods of Irish art. More recently they have measurably concentrated their expertise in the work of the old masters and in twentieth century European art. The gallery has acted on behalf of major museums and works purchased by clients are frequently in demand for international exhibitions. In its nineteenth-century premises in Mount Street, Mayfair, the gallery maintains an elegant, yet convivial ambience in which pictures can be viewed and discussed in a friendly and informed way.

Pyms Gallery

FINE ART DEALERS AND VALUERS

9 Mount Street   Mayfair   London W1K 3NG
Telephone: 020 7629 2020   Facsimile: 020 7629 2060
Email: paintings@pymsgallery.com   www.pymsgallery.com

© Pyms Gallery and authors
June 2001
Edition: 2500

ISBN 0 9525017 7 5

Pyms Gallery
9 Mount Street
Mayfair
London W1K 3NG
Telephone: 020 7629 2020
Facsimile: 020 7629 2060
Email: paintings@pymsgallery.com
www.pymsgallery.com

Design by Peter Gladwin
Photography by Douglas A. Howden
Printed by specialblue, London